Fashion DESIGN SCHOOL *for* KIDS AND TEENS

Fun Activities and Guidance to Start Kids and Teens on Their Fashion Design Journey

FOR AGES 8–14

MADELEINE HUWILER

CONTENTS

Chapter 5. Practice Makes Perfect! 108

Chapter 6. Preparing Your Fashion Week Collection 122

Conclusion 141

Welcome to *Fashion Design School for Kids and Teens*! My name is Madeleine, and I'm a fashion designer working in Paris. I make accessories such as bags, shoes, and jewelry for many famous fashion brands.

I've written this book to help the next generation of fashion designers learn as much as possible about the fashion industry so that one day, they can design their own amazing clothes and accessories!

Join me on this journey as I teach you all about the exciting world of fashion and show you everything you need to get started as a fashion designer of the future.

YOUR FASHION GUIDE

Throughout the pages of this book, you will be guided along the stages of building a career in fashion. You will learn about the different jobs in the fashion industry and how you can bring your designs to life. Each section will include activities to empower you in putting your new skills into practice. This means that you will learn loads of new techniques from drawing and sketching different items of clothing to creating mood boards, choosing colors, drawing figures, and how to bring all of that together to create your own unique designs. Once you have mastered these skills, you will design your very first Fashion Week catwalk collection!

WHAT SUPPLIES YOU'LL NEED

Before we get started on this fashion design journey, you'll need a few supplies to help you along the way. Many of these supplies are just like the ones you use for your regular art projects, so you

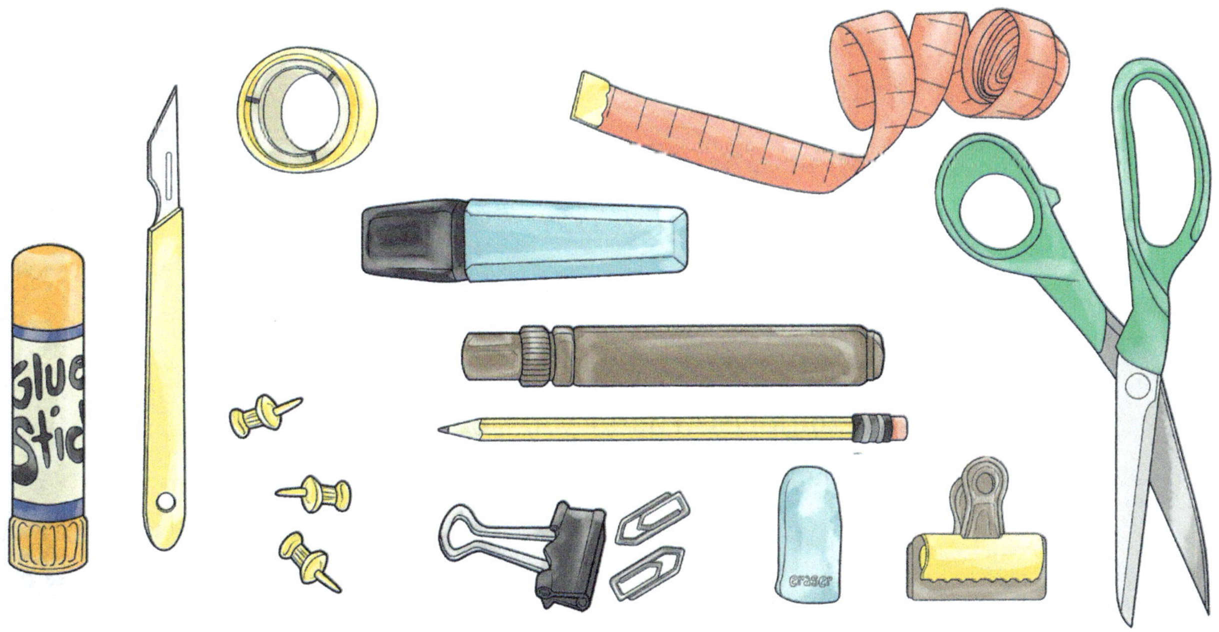

may already have a lot of what you need. Grab your colored pencils, markers, glue, paper, and scissors—these will be your trusty companions throughout the book.

But wait, there's more! As a fashion designer, you'll also be creating mood boards. These are collages that capture the essence of your ideas for your designs. To prepare for creating a stunning mood board, gather some extra materials that inspire you: fabric swatches, trims, buttons, or even images from magazines or photographs that catch your eye. Maybe, you can even become an eco-conscious fashion designer and "upcycle" many of these supplies by getting them from old clothes that you've grown out of. Fabric paints and fabric glue will also help you add your unique flare to your designs.

The last two items you may need along the way are a needle and thread—though only two activities in the book require the use of these, so don't worry if you can't get your hands on them just yet.

With these supplies in hand, you'll be ready to embark on a thrilling fashion design adventure.

01
A LIFE IN
Fashion

In this chapter, we'll discover the exciting journey of how fashion designers take their ideas and convert them into a real clothing collection that is sold in stores. We'll also explore the different jobs available in the fashion industry, explain the difference between fast fashion and luxury fashion, and discuss the importance of sustainability. Lastly, we'll uncover how the fashion calendar works.

Get ready to dive into the very first activities, guiding you as you journey towards becoming an awesome fashion designer. These projects will be right there by your side, offering support and inspiring you as you explore the exciting world of fashion!

THE JOB OF A FASHION *Designer*

WHAT DOES A FASHION DESIGNER DO?

A fashion designer is someone who creates clothes, shoes, and accessories. Fashion designers spend a lot of time researching fashion trends, sketching, and choosing fabrics—all before they start making clothes! They then put all their ideas together to make a design and create a "prototype," which is a sample of the product. This prototype will be seen in fashion magazines and on the catwalk. Once the design is approved for sale, it will be sent to a factory for copies of the design prototype to be produced in many different sizes, all of which end up in shopping malls and the catalogs of online retailers.

HOW DO I BECOME A FASHION DESIGNER?

I bet that you already have some of the skills you would need to become a fully-fledged fashion designer, and even if you don't, you can always start practicing many of them at any time! You don't need any special equipment yet, just a notepad, a pencil, and lots of ideas! First, you need to decide which area of fashion interests you. Do you want to make bags and shoes? Do you love beautiful bridal wear or are you more interested in cozy knitwear? Try sketching some items you'd love to make or wear, and see what you enjoy the most.

It's also important to keep up with the latest fashion trends by reading fashion magazines or browsing your favorite stores in the mall or online.

When you are older, the next step might be to study at a fashion school or intern with an established fashion designer to get some experience. Remember, the most important thing is that you enjoy what you're creating!

Knowing specific words used in the fashion industry is essential. These words will help you understand different types of clothing and accessories, and when you are ready, they will help you talk about and sell your own designs. Ready to level up your style game? Take our awesome quiz, and put your fashion vocabulary to the test.

Try out this fun way to enhance your knowledge and deepen your understanding of fashion terms. Get started now and become a fashion expert!

Connect the words on the left to their meanings on the right.

1. Silhouette

2. Sustainable fashion

3. Statement piece

4. Vintage

5. Street style

6. Embellishment

7. Seamstress

8. Fashion Forecasting

a. Clothing and accessories made with eco-friendly materials and production methods

b. The process of predicting future fashion trends and shopper preferences

c. A person skilled in sewing, particularly in making garments

d. Fashion trends and styles that emerge from urban or street culture

e. Clothing or accessories from a previous era that are considered fashionable and trendy

f. Decorative details added to garments, such as embroidery, sequins, or beads

g. A bold or eye-catching item of clothing or accessory that makes a strong fashion statement

h. The overall shape or outline of a garment

Solutions: 1h / 2e / 3g / 4a / 5d / 6f / 7c / 8b

The Fashion *Design Process*

1. TREND FORECASTING

Fashion forecasting is a bit like predicting the future of fashion: trying to guess what clothes and colors will be popular in the months or even years ahead. This is a vital part of the design process because fashion designers often work on a collection _nine whole months_ in advance! That's because it can take a long time to manufacture clothing or accessories and get everything ready for sale. So, designers work with fashion forecasters

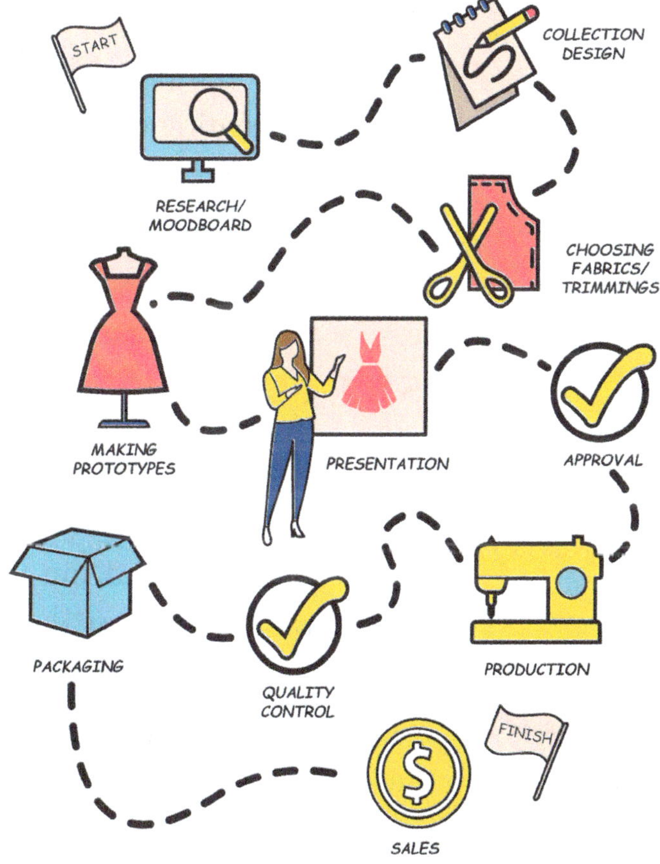

FASHION DESIGN PROCESS

before starting a new collection. Forecasters predict what colors, fabrics, prints, and overall looks will be popular in the upcoming seasons so that designers can make sure their collections are fresh and exciting. It's like having a sneak peek into the future of fashion!

2. RESEARCH

Before fashion designers start drawing their designs, they need to plan and prepare their collections. It's super important! After meeting with the fashion forecaster to see what's going to be popular, designers look for inspiration everywhere: They might read books, check social media, or visit places like art exhibitions or museums. They look for cool ideas that match their themes, such as vintage, ethnic, or contemporary styling. When they find the perfect theme, they start creating a mood board. A mood board is a collage with pictures of things that inspire them, like fabric swatches or photos. It helps designers stay focused and create a collection that matches their vision.

3. SKETCHING THE COLLECTION

Once the fashion designers have their inspiration and ideas, it's time to turn them into sketches. Most designers still like to draw their sketches by hand, but some use digital tools like a computer or tablet. Nowadays, many designers also use 3D programs to create their designs. This allows them to see what their clothes will look like from all angles in 3D. The sketching part of the process is usually the longest, and designers make lots of different sketches. But in the end, they have to choose the best designs and looks to create a collection of garments that tell a visual "story" that matches the decided theme. They need to make sure that the colors, materials, and themes all match and work together. It's kind of like putting together a puzzle!

4. CHOOSING THE PERFECT FABRIC

Choosing the right fabric is a crucial part of the fashion design process. Before creating a prototype, designers carefully consider which fabric will work best for each design. They need to take into account things like the weight, stretch, and quality of the fabric to make sure it will bring out the best in their designs. If they choose the wrong fabric, the garment might not turn out as planned and it could look completely different from what they had envisioned. That's why designers need to be very careful when selecting fabrics. By choosing the perfect fabric for each design, they can make sure their creations look amazing and stand out from the crowd. We'll be learning more about how to make this choice in Chapter 2.

5. CREATING THE PROTOTYPES

A prototype is a special sample garment made by the factory or in the designer's workshop. It's unique and made just for testing! The prototype is fitted on a model to check if the size is correct and comfortable for presentation at fashion shows. During the fitting, the designer and their team check the measurements, fit, and materials to make sure the prototype is as close to the initial design as possible. A technical designer—who is responsible for turning the initial design into a finished product—is also there to help make any changes to the pattern and create the final sample. Prototypes are super important to make sure the final product looks amazing and fits just right!

6. PRESENTATION

Once the prototype is approved, it's time to show the new collection! The fashion designer and their team present the collection to retail buyers and journalists. This can happen at a fashion show, trade show, or presentation. Retail buyers are there to check out the new collection and decide which pieces will become available for sale in their stores. Journalists and other members of the press are there to get information about the new looks and write about them in magazines. It's a super exciting time because all the hard work is finally paying off!

7. PRODUCTION

After the sales events, the fashion designer and their team receive all the orders from retail buyers and stores. Then, it's time to let the factories know how many garments they need to make and explain each garment to the technicians. The patterns used for the prototypes need to be adapted for mass production. Factories can make thousands of garments per

week using high-tech cutting and sewing machines. It's important to make sure everything is perfect because many people will be wearing the clothes!

8. LAUNCHING THE COLLECTION

Once the production is completed, the garments go through a final quality control check before they are shipped to the warehouse for storage. From there, the ordered garments are sent to both brick-and-mortar and online stores to be presented and sold.

It's an exciting moment for the fashion designer and their team who get to see their hard work and creativity displayed in stores for people to enjoy and wear!

9. MARKETING

Marketing and promotion are a crucial part of the fashion process. They help to showcase the designer's creation and vision to the world. Marketing professionals work with the fashion designer to create a photo shoot or video campaign that captures the essence of the collection. These images or videos are then used in the seasonal lookbook, fashion blogs, and websites, or sent to retail buyers and the press. With the help of marketing, the fashion brand can reach a larger audience and build its brand image.

A TEAM EFFORT

As a fashion designer, working as part of a team is really important. Most fashion designers don't work alone; instead, they rely on the help of others to make their vision come to life. In fact, successful fashion designers have many assistants who will do everything from attending trade shows to choosing fabrics, creating mood boards, and helping with design ideas.

Fashion designers often work to tight deadlines, so everyone must work together to prepare everything on time. A good fashion designer needs to be a good communicator, friendly, creative, and enjoy working with others. *Does that sound like you?*

Do you like colors and fabrics? Do clothes in magazines or online inspire you? Do you want to make people happy and confident with your designs? Write down your reasons! It's important to remember why you chose this path, and it can help you stay motivated on your journey to becoming a fashion designer.

OTHER Fashion *Careers*

In the fashion industry, there's a whole world of exciting roles beyond just designing clothes. It's not just about being a fashion designer! There are so many cool jobs that play a vital role in making fashion awesome. Let's explore some of them!

FASHION PHOTOGRAPHERS

Fashion photographers play an important role by creating images for advertising campaigns, catalogs, and fashion magazines. They collaborate closely with fashion designers and groups of designers, called *fashion houses*, to ensure that the pictures accurately reflect the brand's image. Fashion photographers can work in studios or travel to various locations for photo shoots.

FASHION BUYERS

Fashion buyers choose what clothes and accessories will be sold in stores. They need to understand what people want to buy and what styles and colors are trendy. They use this information to create in-store collections that will be popular with customers and earn money for the store. They also need to think about how much money customers will be willing to spend and, therefore, how much the store should charge for each item.

VISUAL MERCHANDISERS

Visual merchandisers are the people who design and arrange the displays in stores and shop windows. Their job is to make the products look as attractive as possible so that people will want to buy them. They use colors, lighting, and other visual elements to create an appealing shopping environment that will grab people's attention and make them want to come inside and have a closer look at the collection.

MAKEUP ARTISTS AND HAIR STYLISTS

For fashion shows, photo shoots, magazines, and video promotions, makeup artists and hair stylists are key members of the crew who prepare models for the event. They work closely with the designer to create a specific look and feel that complements the clothing. At major fashion shows, the work of a makeup artist is crucial in helping models stand out on the runway.

MODELS

Fashion brands use models to showcase their clothing, makeup, and other products in magazines, on runways, and in advertisements. Models work with stylists and makeup artists to create their looks, but they are each responsible for bringing their own unique personality and style to the camera and catwalk.

RETAIL MANAGERS

Retail managers are like captains of a ship. They're responsible for making sure their store is always well-stocked and looks great. They need to make sure the prices are just right and the products are displayed in a way that makes customers want to buy them. They also hire and train staff to provide the best service possible and make sure everyone is happy and working together as a team.

E-COMMERCE MANAGERS

An e-commerce manager for a fashion brand is responsible for managing the online store. They work with the website design team to create an online store that is visually appealing and easy to navigate. The e-commerce manager also ensures that all products are displayed with accurate descriptions and pricing. They may also be responsible for online marketing, such as social media advertising and email campaigns. It is their job to make sure that customers have a great online shopping experience and that the brand is making sales through their e-commerce platform.

STYLISTS

Fashion stylists are like personal shoppers for models and celebrities! They work with designers and clothing brands to pick out the perfect outfits for photo shoots, music videos, and red carpet events. They know all about the latest fashion trends and help make sure everything looks just right!

FASHION JOURNALISTS

Fashion journalism is all about keeping the public up-to-date with the latest fashion trends and styles. Fashion journalists gather information by working with stylists, interviewing fashion designers, and attending fashion shows, photoshoots, and events. They then write articles and create content for fashion magazines, websites, and social media platforms.

SOCIAL MEDIA MANAGERS

Social media is a big part of how fashion brands connect with their fans and customers. Social media managers for fashion brands are responsible for creating and posting photos, videos, and stories on all social media platforms. They also respond to comments and messages and work to build relationships with followers. The goal is to keep fans excited about the brand and interested in its latest products and trends.

Fashion
FROM FAST FASHION TO *Luxury*

WHAT IS FAST FASHION?

Fast fashion is cheap, trendy clothing that is worn for a short amount of time. Fast fashion designers follow trends from celebrities and mass-produce cheap versions as quickly as possible for the big stores. They aren't designed with quality in mind, so they often become damaged (or no longer fashionable) more quickly, causing people to throw them away.

Fast fashion also usually involves hiring workers from poorer countries who have bad working conditions and receive very low pay. Plus, the amount of waste is bad for the environment.

WHAT IS LUXURY FASHION?

Fashion doesn't have to be harmful to other people or the planet. Luxury fashion uses high-quality materials that are designed to last for a long time and are often handmade in small quantities.

Luxury fashion is meant to be "timeless" because it's made to be worn for a long time rather than following short-term trends. As luxury fashion is much more expensive, workers are more regularly paid fairly with good working conditions, but it's always important to check that you know the ethics behind your clothing manufacturer.

Sustainable Fashion
CREATING A GREENER
Future

As a future fashion designer, it's really important to know about sustainable fashion. Sustainability in fashion means meeting the demands of your customers while caring for the planet and reducing the damage that will affect future generations.

Some materials are more sustainable than others: For example, organic cotton uses less water than conventional cotton and avoids harmful chemicals like pesticides. Sustainable fashion brands should also avoid using certain chemicals and dyes in their clothing, which can pollute the local environment and cause damage to the animals that live there.

As online shopping is becoming more and more popular, sustainable brands also need to consider how they package and ship their products.

> *To practice good waste management, brands should consider using recycled materials and avoid over-producing items that could be thrown away.*

UPCYCLING OLD CLOTHES INTO FASHIONABLE SCRUNCHIES!

Don't throw away your old clothes! Let's discover the exciting world of upcycling, where we can transform them into something new and fabulous. In this activity, we'll show you a fantastic idea for upcycling your old t-shirts or sweaters.

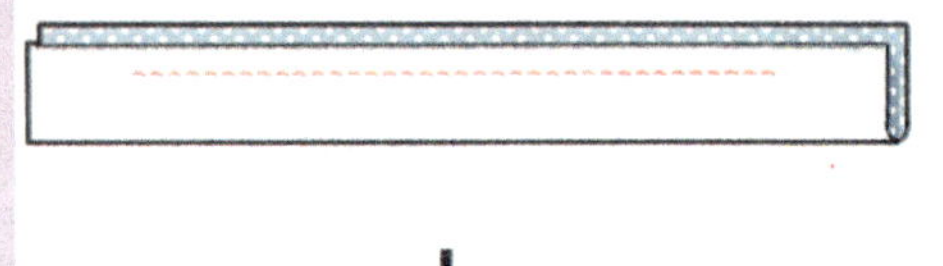

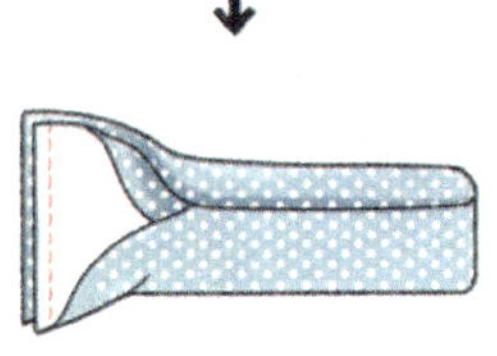

Materials needed:

- old clothes or fabric scraps
- elastic
- a needle
- thread

Instructions:

1. Cut fabric into rectangles (around 4 inches wide and 18 inches long).
2. Fold the rectangular fabric in half lengthwise with the patterned or "good" side of the fabric facing inward.
3. Pin and sew the long edge, leaving the ends open.
4. Turn the created fabric tube right side out.
5. Insert elastic, and sew the ends together to create a loop.
6. Fold and sew the open ends of the fabric tube.
7. Trim excess fabric and threads.
8. Repeat with other fabric pieces.
9. Style and enjoy your fashionable upcycled scrunchies!

Fashion seasons and the fashion calendar play an important role in the fashion industry. There are four main seasons in fashion: spring, summer, fall, and winter. Each season has its own unique fashion trends and styles.

The fashion calendar is a schedule of important fashion events, such as fashion weeks, trade shows, and other fashion-related events. These events are where fashion designers showcase their latest collections.

Fashion weeks happen twice a year, and they're usually held in the major fashion capitals of the world like Paris, New York, Milan, and London. During Fashion Week, designers showcase their latest designs in runway shows, where models walk down the runway wearing the latest fashion trends.

Trade shows are where fashion buyers, retailers, and wholesalers come together to buy and sell fashion products for the upcoming seasons. It's also an opportunity for designers to showcase their collections to potential buyers.

Fashion is always changing; that's why we have seasons in fashion. Each season has its own unique styles and trends, and fashion designers work hard to create new collections for each season. The fashion calendar helps designers plan their collections for important events like Fashion Week. As fashion lovers, it's exciting to see what's new and trending each season and to try out new styles that fit our personal tastes and expression.

The following is a list of questions that can help any budding fashion designer to find their unique style. It's okay if you don't have answers to all of these just yet, but take a moment to think about your fashion dreams, and write down any ideas you do have.

1. What kind of fashion designs do you enjoy creating the most?

2. What will be the name of your brand? Why did you choose this name?

3. Who do you imagine wearing your designs?

4. What is your favorite fashion trend at the moment?

5. Which famous fashion designers do you look up to, and why?

6. What kind of materials do you enjoy working with the most?

7. How do you plan on making your designs sustainable and environmentally friendly?

8. Can you describe your dream fashion show or runway event?

02

DESIGNING A
Collection

Throughout this chapter, you will learn all about creating a fashion collection! We'll show you each step of the way, from finding inspiration to playing with vibrant colors and starting a cool mood board. You'll also learn about fabrics, prints, pattern-making, and the awesome process of turning designs into real, stylish garments.

You will even learn about sewing techniques, find out how to add cool embellishments, and have fun with engaging activities that will guide you through each step.

INSPIRATIONS, Concepts, and Themes

Have you ever wondered where fashion designers get their ideas? Well, it all starts with inspiration and concept!

Inspiration can come from anywhere, such as nature, art, music, and even everyday objects. Fashion designers use their creativity to take these ideas and turn them into unique and beautiful pieces of clothing.

Once they have their inspiration, fashion designers start to develop a concept. A concept is the overall idea that will guide the creation of a collection. It could be a theme, a mood, or even a story. For example, a designer might create a collection inspired by the beach and the ocean. They might choose colors like blues and greens and use lightweight, natural materials like linen and cotton to create a relaxed and breezy vibe.

Fashion designers use their inspiration and concept to create sketches and designs, choose fabrics and colors, and eventually create the final product. It's amazing to see how an idea can turn into a beautiful piece of clothing that we can wear and enjoy.

1. Start by thinking about what you've seen people wearing lately. Have you noticed any trends or patterns? What do you think might be the basis for these trends? For instance, are bright colors trendy because it is sunny most days? Maybe, people are turning to cozy knitwear to get them through the winter.

2. Go to different places like your school or the mall, or look through fashion magazines or websites to spot new trends.

3. Write down what you see, and make notes about why you think people are making those choices. This will enable you to think ahead to what might be trendy in the next season. For example, will cargo pants be in fashion again? What color do you think will be popular?

4. Don't be afraid to be creative and think outside the box—sometimes the most interesting trends come from unexpected places!

5. Once you're done trendspotting and forecasting, write down your ideas below.

6. Use your ideas to inspire your own fashion designs.

Tend #1:

Tend #2:

Tend #3:

EXPLORING *Colors* AND PALETTES

Colors are a big part of fashion! From the clothes we wear to the accessories we choose, colors play an important role in making a fashion statement. Understanding how colors work together is important for fashion design. Let's learn about the basics of color and how you can create a color palette to make a stylish fashion collection!

THE BASICS OF COLOR

Color is created by light and how it interacts with objects. When light hits an object, it is either absorbed, reflected, or transmitted. The color we see is determined by the type of light that is reflected back to our eyes. For example, a red apple appears red because it reflects red light and absorbs all other colors.

There are three primary colors: red, yellow, and blue. These colors cannot be created by mixing other colors together. Secondary colors are created by mixing two primary colors together. For example, mixing yellow and blue creates the secondary color green. Tertiary colors are created by mixing a primary color with a secondary color. For example, mixing red with orange creates red-orange. How colors interact with one another can be displayed on the color wheel—an excellent tool for designers who are deciding on color palettes.

A color palette is a group of colors that go well together. Choosing the right colors is important in fashion design because it can create different moods and feelings.

There are four types of color palettes: monochromatic, analogous, complementary, and triadic. A *monochromatic* palette uses different shades of one color. *Analogous* colors are next to each other on the color wheel. *Complementary* colors are opposite each other on the wheel, and *triadic* colors are evenly spaced. By understanding color palettes, fashion designers can create beautiful and stylish outfits that evoke the mood they want.

Color Wheel

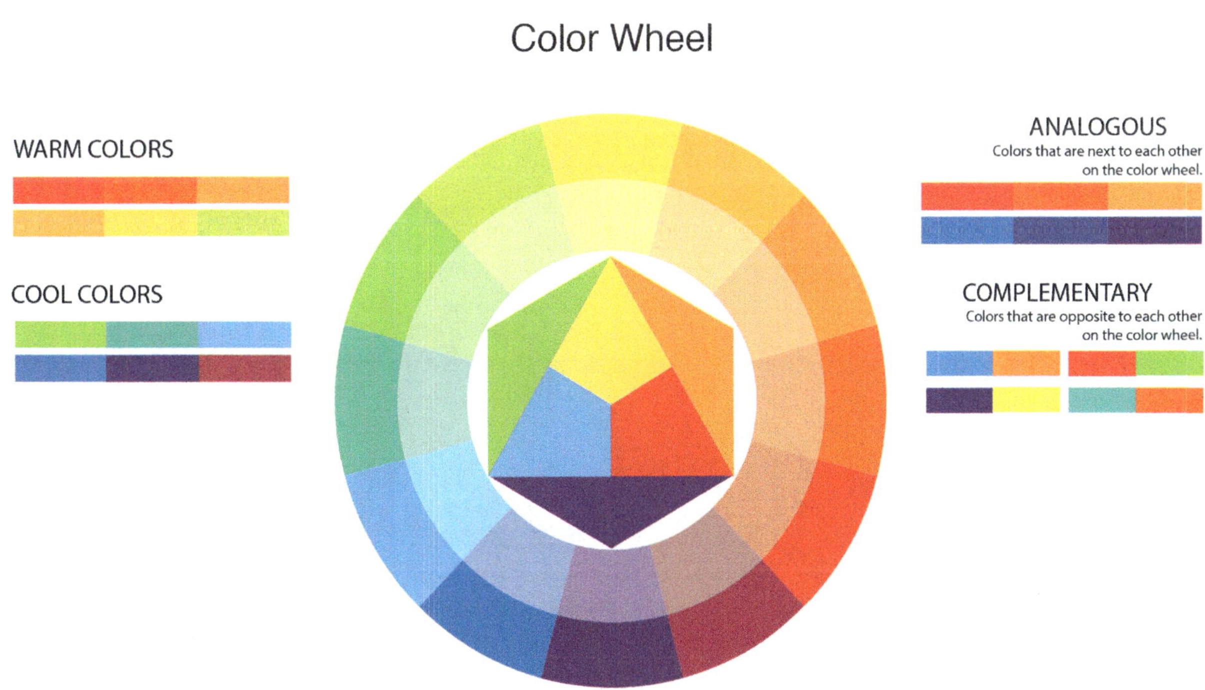

In this activity, you'll create your own color palette for a fashion collection. Start by selecting a main color, and then choose two or three additional colors that work well with it. You can use the color wheel to help you select colors that work well together.

COLOR PALETTE #1

COLOR PALETTE #2

COLOR PALETTE #3

Creating A MOOD BOARD

Mood boards are a fun and creative way to explore fashion and develop your own unique sense of style. A mood board is a collage of images, textures, and colors that capture a certain mood or theme. In fashion, mood boards are often used by designers and stylists to gather inspiration and create a visual representation of their ideas before starting the collection.

Let's make your own mood board. Here are some tips to get you started:

1 Choose a theme: Before you start collecting images, think about what kind of mood or theme you want your mood board to convey. It could be a color scheme, a particular style (such as vintage or bohemian), or even a specific character or era.

2 Collect images: Once you have a theme in mind, start collecting images that fit that theme. You can find pictures in magazines, on the internet, or even take your own photos. Look for images of clothes, accessories, textures, patterns, and colors that inspire you.

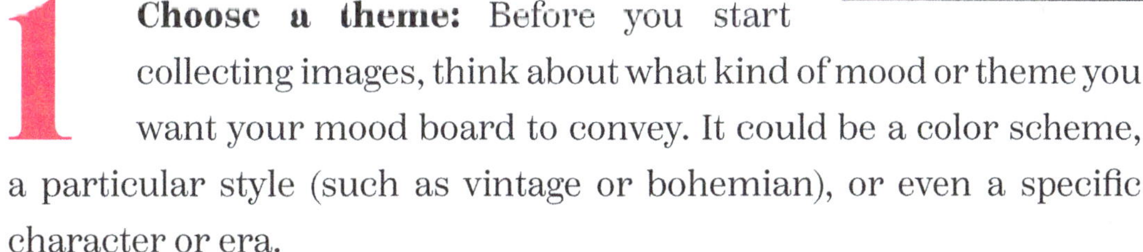

3   **Arrange your images:** Once you have a collection of images, start arranging them on a piece of paper or poster board. Try different layouts and combinations until you find a composition that feels balanced and visually interesting. You can use glue or tape to attach your images to the board.

4   **Add text and other elements:** If you want to add more visual interest to your mood board, try adding text or other elements. You could write out quotes or descriptions of your favorite styles or add embellishments like sequins or ribbons.

5   **Display your mood board:** Once you've completed your mood board, display it somewhere where you can see it often, such as on your bedroom wall or in your closet. Use it as a source of inspiration when you're putting together outfits, shopping for new clothes, or sketching your own designs.

Remember, a mood board is all about capturing a certain mood or feeling, so don't worry too much about making it perfect.

FABRICS & MATERIALS

Fabrics and materials are essential components of fashion design. Designers use a variety of fabrics to create different types of clothing, accessories, and footwear. Some of the most common fabrics used in fashion include cotton, silk, wool, polyester, and denim.

Cotton is a popular fabric because it's soft, breathable, and versatile. It's used to create everything from t-shirts to dresses, and it is a staple in many people's wardrobes.

Silk is a luxurious fabric that's known for its soft and shiny texture. It's often used in formal wear, such as evening gowns and ties.

Wool is a warm and durable fabric that's commonly used in coats, jackets, and suits. It comes in different weights and textures, making it a versatile option for designers. However, it is very sensitive to shrinkage and must be washed carefully.

Polyester is a synthetic fabric that's popular because it's affordable, easy to care for, and comes in a variety of colors and patterns. It's often used in casual wear, such as t-shirts and athletic wear.

Denim is a durable and versatile fabric that's often used in jeans, jackets, and skirts. It comes in different colors, making it a popular choice for both casual wear and workwear for manual laborers.

In addition to these fabrics, designers also use a variety of other materials such as leather, fur, and synthetic materials like PVC and nylon.

> *By choosing the right fabric and material, designers can create clothing and accessories that are not only fashionable but also functional and comfortable to wear.*

In addition to these commonly used fabrics, there's another exciting option to consider: ecological fabrics. These fabrics are made from sustainable materials, which means they are better for the environment. For example, organic cotton is grown without harmful chemicals, and hemp-based fabrics require less water to produce. By choosing ecological fabrics, we can make a positive impact and promote a greener fashion industry.

This fun and educational activity will help you develop your senses and learn more about the fabrics and materials used in fashion.

Materials needed:

- A selection of garments that you can find at home, such as t-shirts, skirts, bags, coats, or bathing suits.

Instructions:

1. Gather a selection of garments. Make sure you choose a variety of clothing with different textures and properties, such as being soft, rough, smooth, or shiny.

2. Place each garment on a table, and feel the fabric with your hands. Try to guess what kind of fabric it is made of based on its texture, thickness, and appearance.

3. Write down your guess for each garment on a piece of paper.

4. Once you have made all your guesses, check the washing tag on each garment to see if you were correct.

5. Compare your guesses with the actual fabric composition of each garment. Did you guess correctly? Were there any surprises?

FASHION DESIGN SKETCHES

Fashion design sketches are an important part of the fashion design process. They allow designers to plan and visualize their ideas before creating a physical garment. A sketch is a drawing that shows the basic structure, shape, material, and details of a design.

Sketches can be created using various materials such as pencils, markers, or digital tools like tablets or computers. Designers often use *croquis*—which are templates of fashion figures— to accurately draw the human body and create well-fitting designs.

When creating a fashion design sketch, it's important to consider the details of the garment, such as the silhouette, the fabric, and any embellishments or accessories.

Fashion design sketches are not only essential for designers, but they can also be a fun way to express creativity and explore different fashion styles.

In Chapter 3, you will discover more about how to create fashion design sketches using croquis. For now, why not experiment and have fun with a croquis of your own?

It's time to try out your first fashion design! Use the croquis provided to sketch your first look. Don't worry if it's not perfect, it's just a first trial. You will learn more about how to draw and refine your sketches later in this book.

PRINT DESIGN

In fashion, the word "print" refers to the patterns or designs that are added to the fabric of a garment. Different types of prints include floral, animal, geometric, and many more. Printing is an important part of the textile industry. Just like dyeing, printing can make clothes look colorful and interesting.

There are several ways to create print patterns. Some of the most common methods include screen printing, digital printing, block printing, and hand painting. Each method has its own unique process and produces different results, giving designers a range of options to choose from when creating their designs.

WHAT IS A REPEAT PRINT?

When textile designers create printed fabrics, they use a technique called *repeats*. This means they make sure that the pattern on the fabric matches up at the edges and continues perfectly without any gaps. The point where the design starts again is called a repeat. The purpose of using repeats is to make the fabric look like it goes on forever without stopping. Textile designers have been using repeats for a long time, and today, with digital technology, they can make all sorts of different repeats. Repeats are not just used in fabric design, they're also used in other things like wallpaper.

Activity

CREATE A REPEAT PRINT

Create four unique print designs and experiment with various print motifs such as flowers, geometric patterns, graffiti, and more.

WHAT ARE PLACEMENT PRINTS?

Placement prints are a great way of printing designs on garments like t-shirts or dresses. Unlike regular prints that repeat all over, placement prints are placed in a specific spot. Designers use specially sized artwork and design it in a unique way to create awesome prints, just like the T-shirt design below!

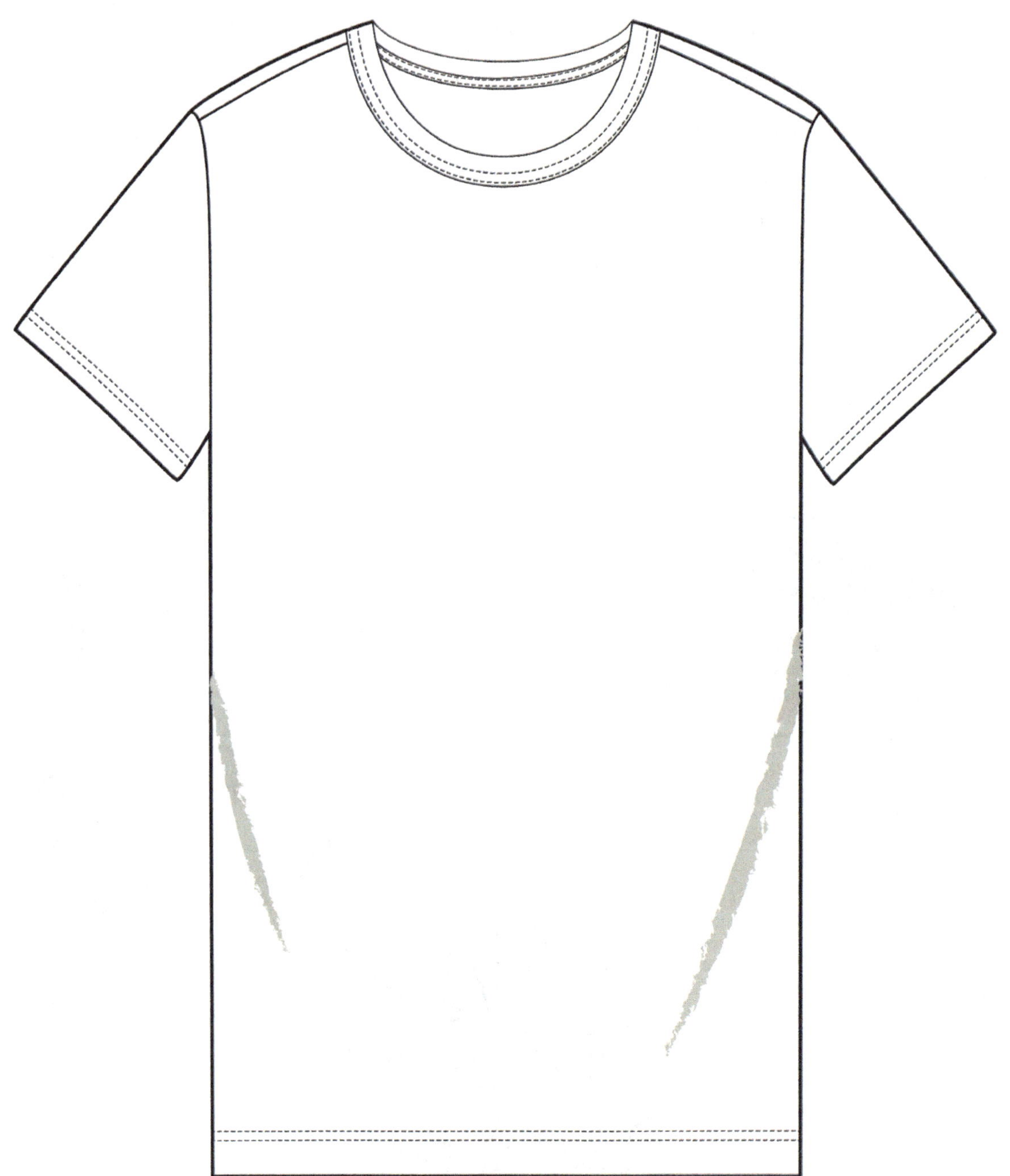

PATTERN-MAKING AND *Draping*

Pattern-making is a technique that fashion designers use to create a blueprint, or "pattern," for their designs. This pattern is used to cut fabric into the right shape for a garment, making sure it fits correctly and looks great. There are two types of patterns: flat patterns and draping patterns.

Flat patterns are made on paper or cardboard and are great for creating patterns for different sizes of garments. Designers take measurements, draw the design, and add seam allowances—extra space to allow the fabric pieces to be sewn together—to make sure the final garment fits perfectly. Draping patterns, on the other hand, involve shaping fabric directly on a mannequin or dress form. This allows designers to experiment with different fabrics, colors, and shapes and create unique, one-of-a-kind pieces that can't be replicated with paper patterns.

Draping is like sculpting with fabric. Designers can mold the fabric into new shapes and designs, which gives them more creative freedom and allows them to make changes to the fabric as they work. It's an exciting technique that helps designers bring their ideas to life in a way that's both practical and creative.

In conclusion, pattern-making and draping are both essential techniques that every fashion designer should know. They form the foundation of understanding tailoring and fashion design.

To gain a better understanding of how draping works in fashion, you can begin by experimenting with fabric on a fashion figure. Here's a simple activity to help you get started.

Materials you'll need:

- White paper
- Pens, colored pencils, and markers
- Fabric glue
- Fabric swatches, wool, feathers, or other materials of your choice

Instructions:

1. Start by copying one of the fashion figure templates provided in this book onto a separate piece of paper. This will serve as your canvas.

2. Begin exploring different ways to position and drape the fabric swatches on your fashion figure. Consider what silhouettes and trends you noticed during your fashion forecasting, and apply that knowledge to create a dress or skirt.

3. Once you're satisfied with your arrangement, carefully glue the fabric onto the paper, securing it in place. Be mindful of the placement, and ensure it aligns with your envisioned design.

4. To complete your look, add finishing touches such as accessories, hairstyles, and other details that will enhance your fashion creation.

Embellishments

Embellishment is an important part of fashion design. It adds style and personality to clothes and accessories.

There are many different techniques for embellishment, including decorative stitching (known as *embroidery*), beading, patchwork, and fabric painting. Whether using pre-made lacework or making your own trim, the possibilities are endless when it comes to embellishing fabrics. While many embellishing techniques are still done by hand, there are also innovative technologies available to recreate these effects on an industrial scale.

So why not try it out and see what you can create?

LET'S CREATE PERSONALIZED FABRIC PATCHES!

Materials needed:

- Fabric scraps or plain fabric
- Scissors
- Fabric glue or iron-on adhesive
- Fabric markers or paints
- Decorative items like buttons, sequins, or beads

Instructions:

1. Cut out any desired shape from the fabric.

2. Decorate the fabric patch with fabric markers or paints.

3. Add extra flair with embroidery thread or sew-on decorations.

4. Attach buttons, sequins, or beads using fabric glue or iron-on adhesive.

5. Let it dry completely or follow heat-setting instructions.

6. To use the patch as an embellishment, attach it to an item of clothing or accessory using glue or by sewing it on.

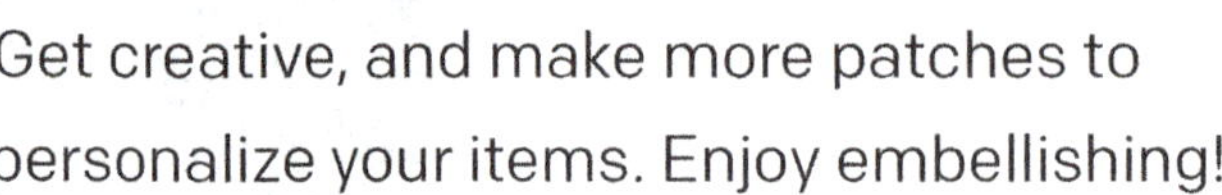

Get creative, and make more patches to personalize your items. Enjoy embellishing!

CONSTRUCTION AND *Sewing*

Sewing and construction are fundamental techniques that every fashion designer should master. These techniques are used to turn flat pieces of fabric into a three-dimensional garment. The construction process starts by cutting the fabric according to the pattern, or design blueprint, and then sewing the pieces together.

There are many steps involved in sewing and constructing a garment, including selecting the right fabric, measuring and cutting the pieces, and using a sewing machine to stitch the fabric together. The stitches must be even and precise to ensure that the garment is sturdy and well-constructed.

Once the garment is sewn together, it goes through a process called finishing, which includes adding any necessary closures such as buttons or zippers, hemming (or turning in) edges to prevent the fabric from fraying, and pressing or ironing the garment to make it look neat and crisp.

Sewing and construction techniques are not only used by fashion designers but also by factories that produce clothing on a larger scale. These factories use specialized machines and equipment to sew garments quickly and efficiently, but the basic principles of sewing and construction are the same.

Becoming a skilled fashion designer involves learning various techniques of sewing and garment construction, understanding how garments are made, and appreciating what it takes to create a well-made piece of clothing. Whether you want to create unique pieces or pursue a career in the fashion industry, mastering these techniques is essential.

Take an old t-shirt you're not using anymore, and give it a new purpose for this activity.

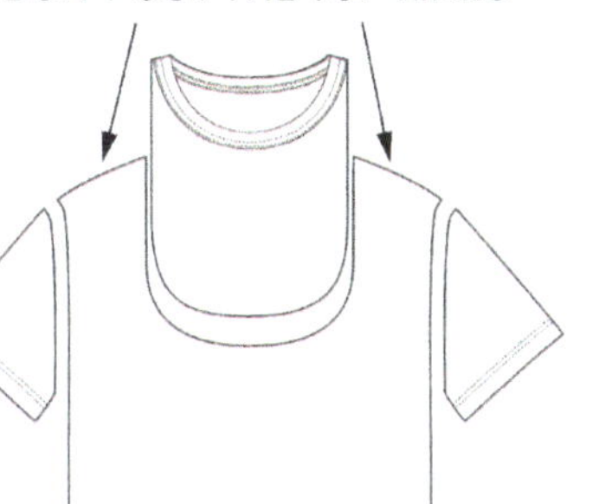

1 Carefully cut the sleeves and the neckline of the t-shirt as shown. Remember to keep the seams on top intact, as they will serve as the handles for your new tote bag!

2 If you have a sewing machine, simply stitch the bottom part together. Alternatively, you can also do this by hand using a thick thread. Make sure to sew tightly and keep the stitches close together to secure the bottom of the tote bag.

3 Your tote bag is complete. If you'd like, you can add a cool print or embellishment to it, just as you learned in the previous activities.

03

INTRODUCTION TO
FASHION DESIGN
Drawing

First, we'll introduce you to the essential tools and materials needed to draw fashion designs. From pencils and markers to sketchbooks and fashion templates, we'll cover everything you need to get started.

We'll also explore the importance of body diversity in fashion. You'll learn how to draw fashion figures of different shapes, sizes, and genders, celebrating the beauty of individuality.

Drawing male, female, and kid's fashion figures is a must-know skill, and we'll guide you step by step, so you can learn all the secrets of proportions, poses, and capturing different styles and personalities.

Are you ready? Let's jump into the world of fashion and start creating!

MATERIALS

Fashion drawing is a way to bring your ideas out of your head and onto paper, which will enable you to communicate your designs with others. To get started with fashion drawing, there are a few tools that you will need.

First, you'll need some good-quality paper. Ideally, fashion designers look for paper that's thick enough to handle different types of drawing materials, such as markers and pencils. You can find sketchpads at most art supply stores, or you get started with any paper that you have on hand in the meantime.

Next, you'll need some drawing tools. Pencils are a great place to start. They come in a variety of hardness levels, from soft to hard, and can be used to create different effects in your drawings. You'll also want to invest in a set of markers, which can help you add color and dimension to your designs.

Other useful tools include rulers and stencils, which can help you create straight lines and precise shapes. You may also want to consider getting a lightbox, which can help you trace your designs onto different sheets of paper.

Remember, fashion drawing is all about expressing your creativity and unique vision. Don't be afraid to experiment with different tools and materials to find what works best for you. With practice and patience, you'll be on your way to creating beautiful fashion designs in no time!

Body Diversity *in Fashion*

Body diversity means that all bodies are different, and there is no such thing as a "perfect" body. Diversity in fashion is very important so that everyone can feel represented and good in their clothes. A fashion designer's job is to make sure that their designs consider different body types and that people of every size, race, gender, and ability are represented.

Fashion design tip:

When you design your clothes, imagine different body types that might wear them. Fashion designers can empower people through their work. Ask yourself, *How can I make people feel good through my designs?*

FASHION FIGURE *Drawing*

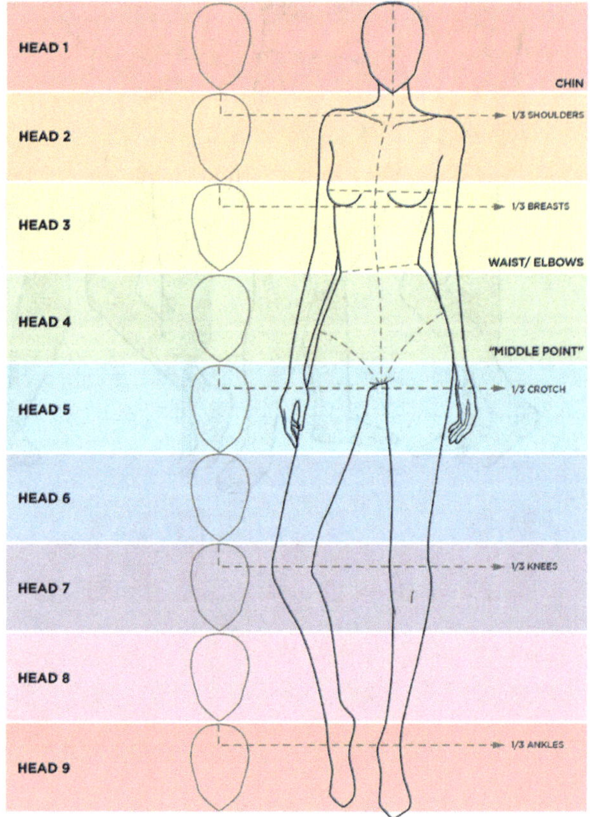

Fashion figure drawing is all about creating a special drawing of a person that will be used as a guide for designing clothing. The basic figure is often made longer than a real person, with certain parts exaggerated to show as many aspects of the design as possible on one sheet of paper. Designers need to know about anatomy, proportions, and balance to get the figure right.

When drawing a fashion figure, designers often use a technique called the "9-head croquis." This means that a fashion figure is drawn to be nine heads tall instead of the usual 7.5–8 heads used when drawing a real person. This makes the figure look more dramatic and allows the designer to play around with the details of the design.

But it's important to remember that this is just a starting point and not a rule. In the fashion industry, there are many different body types and shapes, and it's essential to reflect that in our work. As designers, we have a responsibility to show the diversity that exists in our world and celebrate it through our design.

Fashion Croquis

The best fashion designers draw their own fashion figures rather than working with templates, and since you are well on your way to becoming one of those designers, it is vital that we teach you how to draw your very own fashion figure! It's important to know that learning this might take some time, but don't worry, practice makes perfect. If you find it a bit challenging, you can still use the templates that we provide to help you sketch your designs while you perfect your croquis.

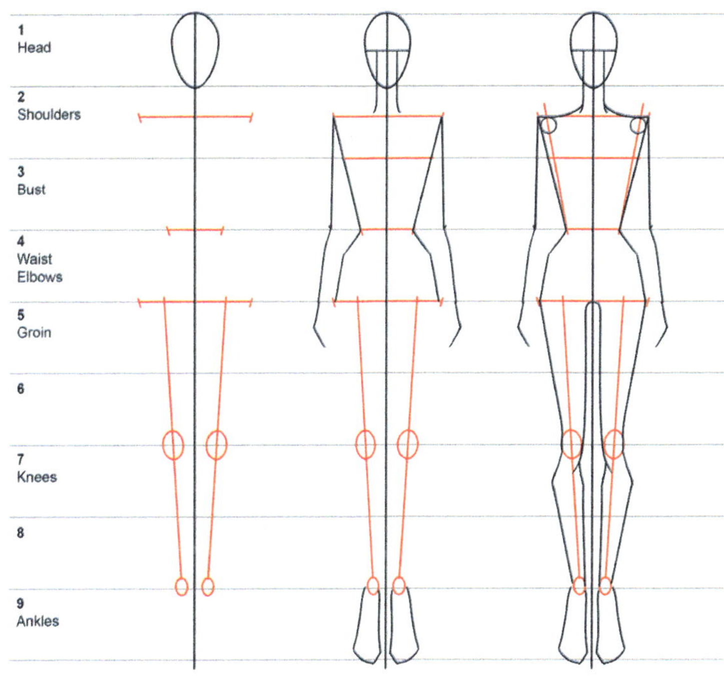

A step-by-step guide on how to build your first 9-heads figure:

1. Draw light lines to separate your page into 9 equal parts, and number them from 1 to 9.

2. Draw an egg shape for the head in between lines 1 and 2.

3. Draw the shoulder line just above the middle of the second segment, and mark the waistline on line 4 with a thinner width.

4. Draw a hip line in line 5, and set the hip width approximately equal to the shoulder width.

5. For placement of the knees, draw small circles on line 7, and then, mark even smaller circles for the ankles on line 9. Connect them with a vertical line up to the hip line to build the structure of the legs.

6. Using what you have already drawn as a framework, flesh out the chest, arms, and hands, keeping in mind the proportions of the body.

7. Connect the hips, knees, and feet with curved lines to create the legs.

8. Draw the feet extending from the ankle structure circles, as shown below.

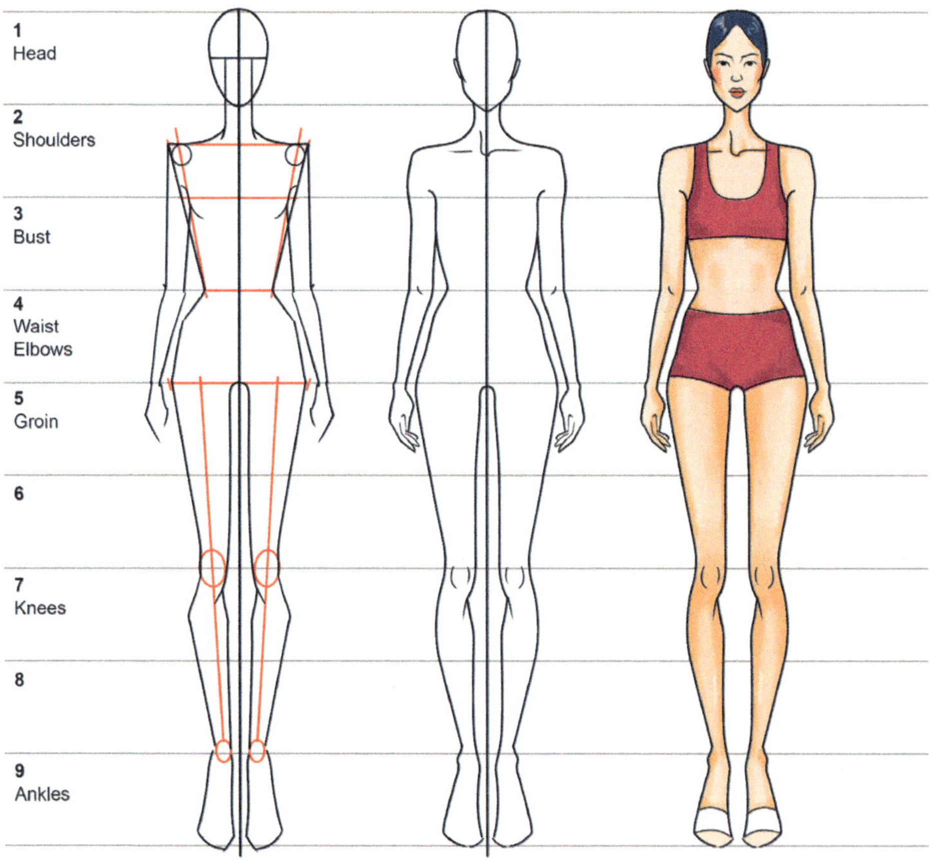

   FASHION DESIGN SCHOOL FOR KIDS AND TEENS

EXPLORING DIFFERENT
FASHION POSES

Not every fashion figure pose works with every outfit. It's important to understand that different types of clothing require different poses to showcase their unique style. For example, a wedding dress design figure would have a different pose than a streetwear look.

To practice drawing different poses in fashion, there are some helpful

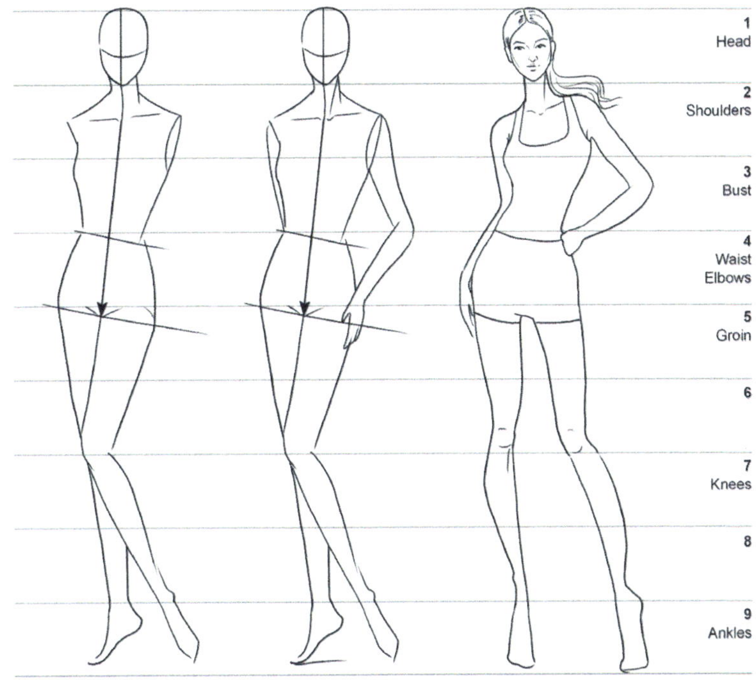

techniques you can try. One method is to print out a photo or use a tablet to trace the main lines of the figure. These lines include the middle line, hip line, waistline, and shoulder line. Drawing these lines helps you understand the body's movements and make it easier to create poses that look natural and dynamic.

On the following pages, you'll find a variety of fashion figures. You can start by trying to copy these figures, paying attention to their proportions and poses. Once you feel comfortable, feel free to create your own fashion figures, adding your personal touch and style.

Keep practicing—it takes time and effort, but it's worth it!

DRAW A FEMALE FASHION FIGURE

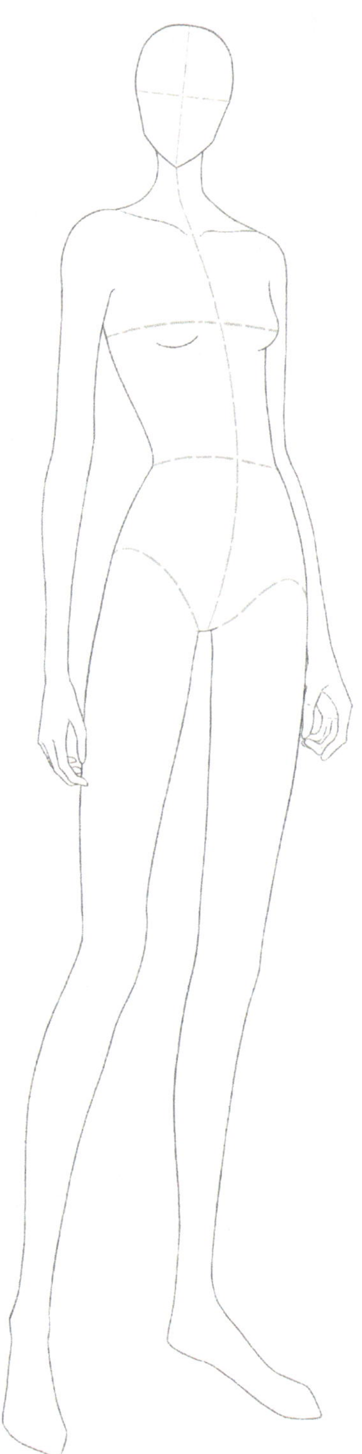

DRAW A MALE FASHION FIGURE

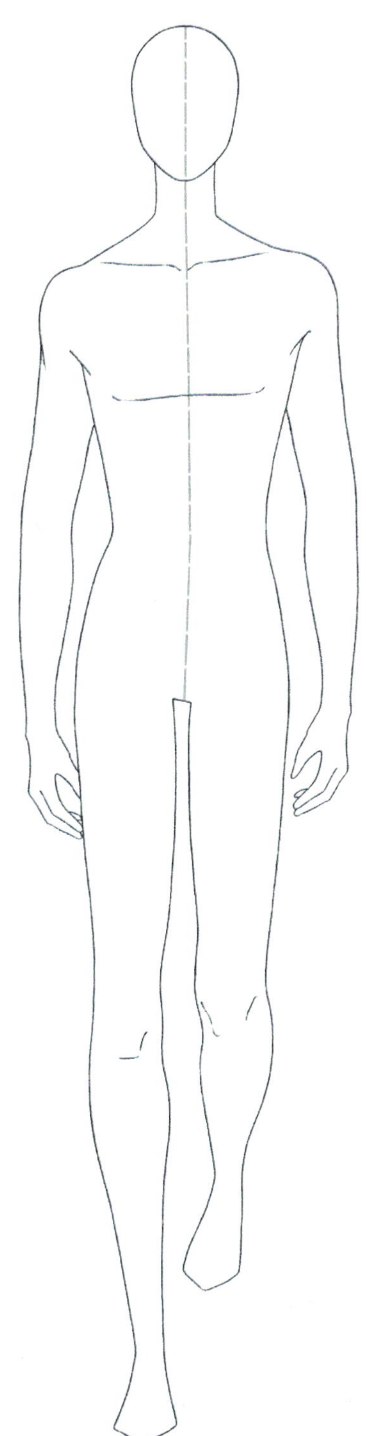

KID'S Fashion Figures

Drawing a children's fashion figure is just like drawing a regular person but with a few key adjustments. Kids have different proportions compared to adults, and it's important to capture their unique charm and energy in your designs. The heads of kids are bigger in relation to their bodies, and their arms and legs are shorter.

One of the main differences between adult and kids' fashion figures is the clothing. Kids' fashion is all about fun, vibrant colors, and playful patterns.

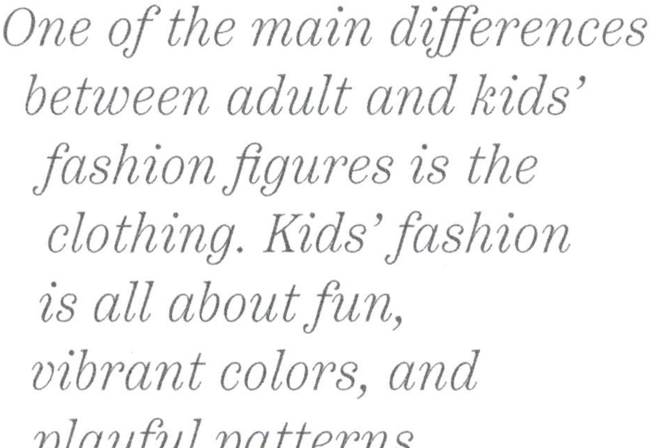

On the following page, you'll find one kids' fashion figure template awaiting your creative touch. So, grab your pencils and get ready to sketch some cool outfits!

DRAW A KIDS' FASHION FIGURE
AND ADD A COOL LOOK

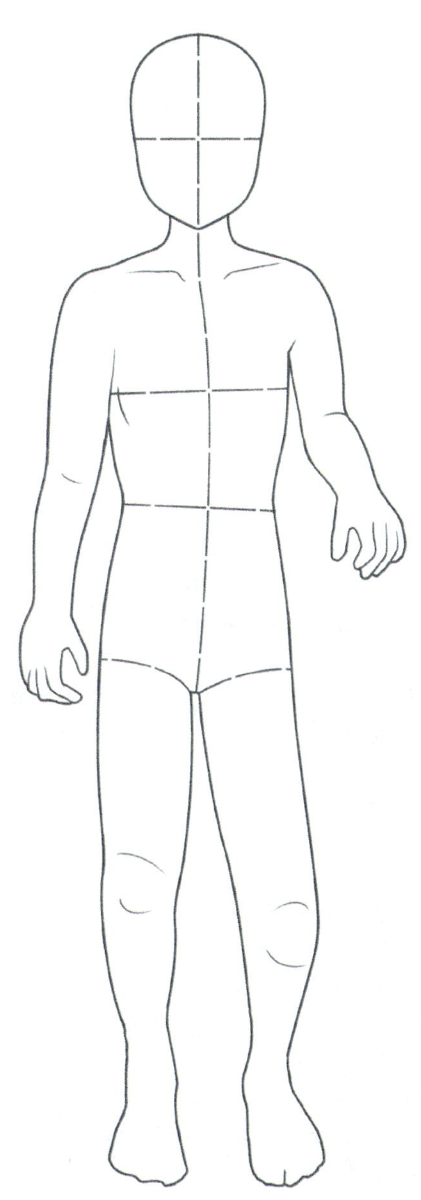

04

Drawing
CLOTHES AND ACCESSORIES

Now that you know how to draw a basic figure, it's time to get creative and draw some awesome clothes! In this chapter, we'll explore different types of clothing and the different styles that you can draw. Pay attention to the shape and purpose of each piece of clothing you're drawing.

Don't worry too much about getting all the details perfect right away. Start by drawing the basic outline of the garment, and then, add details like fabric folds and designs.

Most importantly, don't forget to add your own creative touch to make your designs stand out. Let's get started and have some fun creating awesome fashion designs!

FROM **FASHION CROQUIS** TO THE **FINAL DESIGN**

When creating a fashion design, it's important to know how to apply clothes to a fashion figure template. Start by selecting the clothing you want to draw and gathering reference images to help guide your drawing.

Next, use the fashion figure template as a guide to draw the basic shape of the clothing. Remember to pay attention to the curves of the body and how they affect the way the clothing sits on the figure.

After you've drawn the basic shape of the clothing, it's time to add the details. This can include buttons, pockets, seams, and any other unique features of the clothing. Pay attention to the scale of the details, and make sure they look proportional to the size of the garment and the figure.

When coloring in the clothing, use shading techniques to give the clothing depth and dimension. This can include shading for folds, wrinkles, and areas of shadow.

Remember, the key to designing clothes on a fashion figure template is practice!

Mastering Shape
IN FASHION DESIGN

When it comes to fashion, shape is an important aspect of designing clothes. It helps create different styles and looks that express different moods and personalities. A shape that you might have heard of is the A-line, also known as the "fit and flare." This shape is often seen in dresses, skirts, and coats.

The A-line shape is called that because it looks like the letter A. It starts with a fitted bodice that goes around the chest and waist and then flares out from the waist to create a wide hemline. This shape is often flattering for people who have wider hips and thighs because it draws attention away from those areas and creates a balanced look.

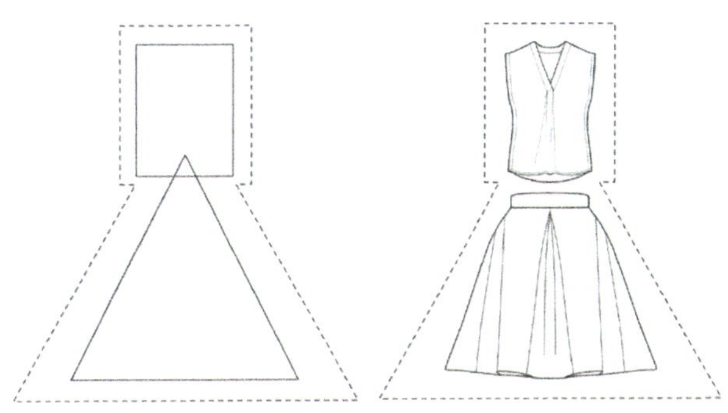

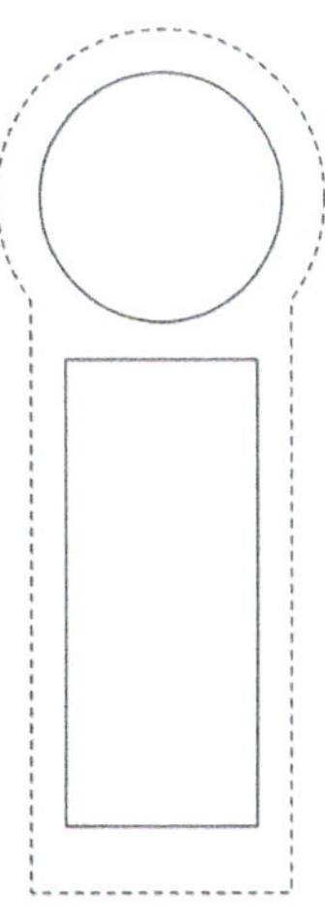

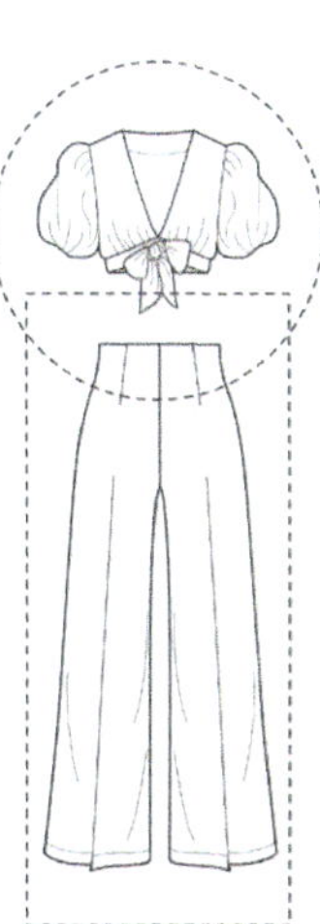

Another popular shape is the sheath or "pencil," which is a straight and narrow style that hugs the body. This is often used in formal dresses and office wear since it is a classic and elegant shape. The ballgown, on the other hand, is a big, poofy skirt that creates a dramatic and glamorous look. This shape is perfect for fancy occasions like proms and weddings.

> *Overall, shape is an essential part of fashion design. It can help create different styles and looks that express unique personalities and moods. So, whether you prefer an A-line, sheath, ballgown, or mermaid silhouette, there's a shape out there that can help you look and feel your best.*

1. Choose one of the fashion shapes mentioned in the text above, such as the A-line, sheath, ballgown, or mermaid silhouette.

2. Sketch your own design of a garment with that shape in mind. You can add any details or embellishments that you like.

3. Once you've finished your sketch, label your design with the name of the shape you chose.

4. Challenge yourself to create as many different designs as you can using that shape, each with its own unique style and details.

HOW TO SKETCH *a Dress*

STEP 1: SKETCH THE SHAPE

Decide on the overall shape of your dress. Will it be fitted, flowing, or structured? Lightly sketch the basic outline as the foundation of your design.

STEP 2: ADD DETAILS

Add character and uniqueness to your dress. Choose the neckline, sleeves, and any special elements that will make it stand out. Get creative with asymmetrical designs, intriguing cutouts, or intricate patterns.

STEP 3: CHOOSE YOUR FABRICS

Explore different fabric choices to bring your dress to life. Imagine it in luxurious satin, flowing chiffon, or textured tweed.

Consider how each fabric will drape and behave, and incorporate those details into your sketch for a realistic touch.

STEP 4: PLAY WITH COLORS

Now, it's time to bring your design to life with colors! Select a palette that suits your dress style and mood. Will you go for bold and vibrant shades or soft and muted tones? Use shading and highlighting techniques to add depth and dimension to your sketch.

Enjoy the journey of creating your unique and stunning dress design!

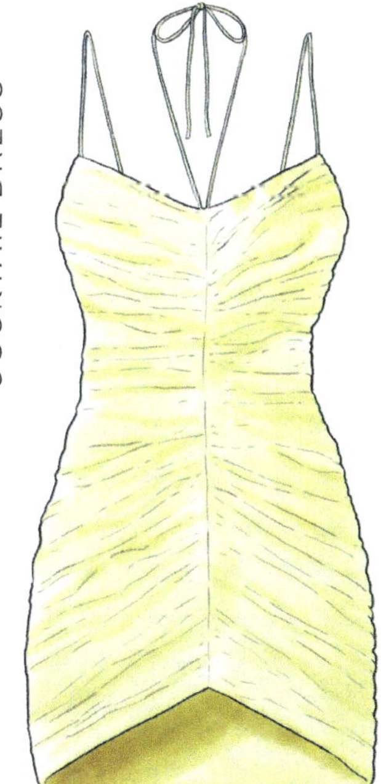

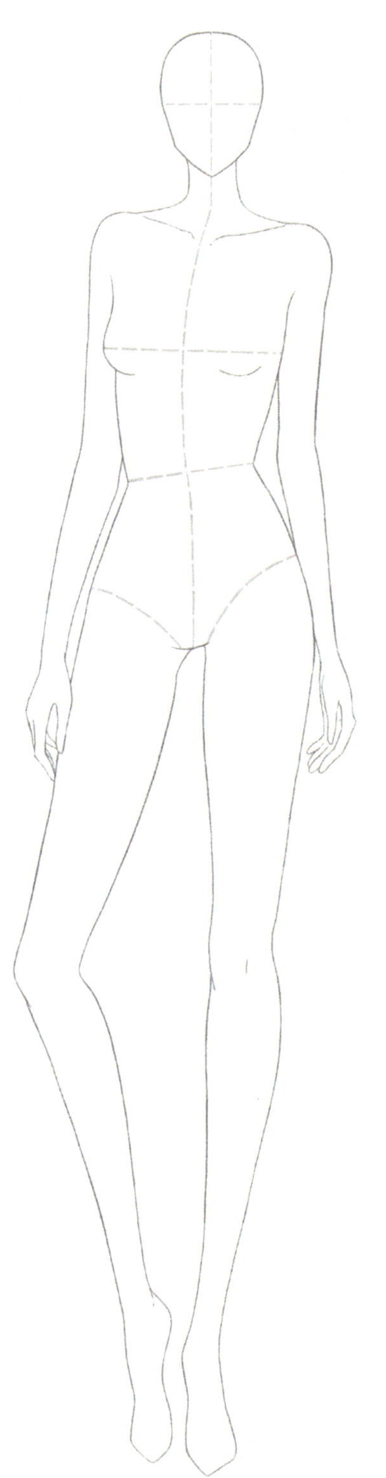

HOW TO SKETCH
A T-SHIRT OR SWEATER

Let's use a hoodie as an example.

STEP 1: START WITH THE BASIC SHAPE

Sketch the outline of the hoodie, focusing on its relaxed and comfortable silhouette.

STEP 2: ADD UNIQUE DESIGN ELEMENTS

Make your hoodie design special by adding details like a drawstring hood, a kangaroo pocket, or ribbed cuffs and hem. Experiment with different sleeve lengths or styles to give it your personal touch.

STEP 3: CONSIDER FABRIC AND TEXTURE

Think about the fabric you want for your hoodie. Will it be cozy fleece or lightweight jersey?

STEP 4: FOCUS ON THE FINER DETAILS

Pay attention to the smaller elements that make each hoodie unique. Consider adding a logo or graphic print, or decide on the placement of extra pockets or embellishments.

STEP 5: REFINE AND FINALIZE

Review your sketch and make any adjustments. Add shading, highlights, or patterns to bring your design to life and show the fabric's texture.

Now, you're ready to create amazing hoodie designs of your own!

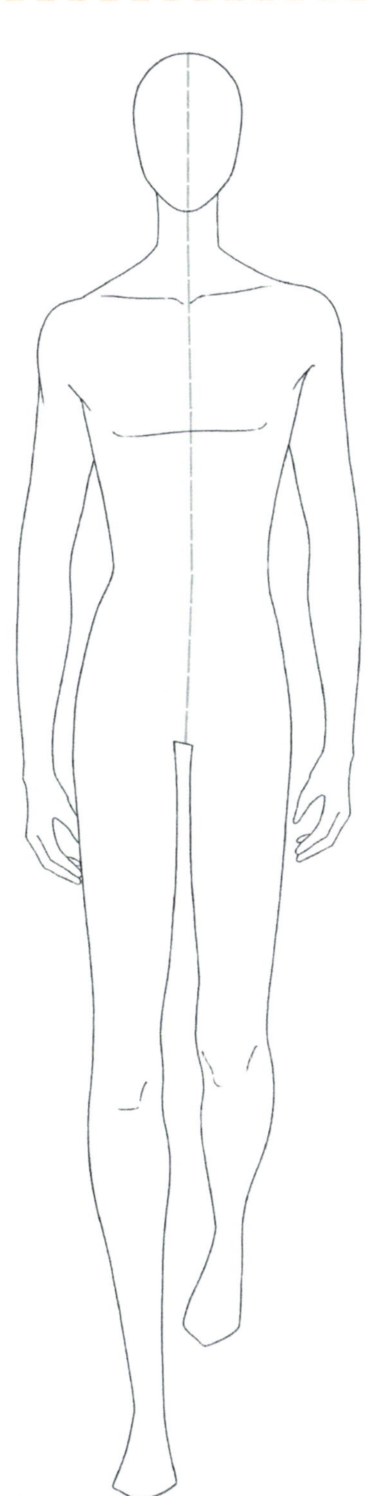

HOW TO SKETCH *Skirts*

STEP 1: START WITH THE BASIC SILHOUETTE

Begin by sketching the outline of your skirt. Decide on the overall shape and length, like a flowing maxi skirt or a sleek pencil skirt. This sets the foundation for your design.

STEP 2: ADD UNIQUE DESIGN ELEMENTS

Make your skirt stand out with special details. Consider a waistband, belt loops, or decorative buttons. Try different pleats, ruffles, or asymmetrical hemlines to add personality.

STEP 3: CONSIDER FABRIC AND TEXTURE

Think about the fabric you want for your skirt. Will it be lightweight like chiffon or textured like tweed? Use shading to show how it drapes and give your sketch a realistic look.

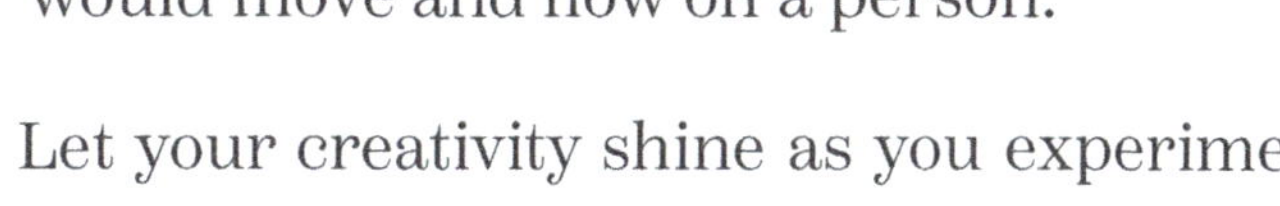

STEP 4: FOCUS ON THE FINER DETAILS

Pay attention to the smaller elements that make your skirt unique. Add trims, lace accents, or embroidery for elegance. Don't forget about closures like zippers or buttons, and think about pockets if needed.

STEP 5: REFINE AND FINALIZE

Add shading, highlights, or patterns to bring your design to life. Imagine how the skirt would move and flow on a person.

Let your creativity shine as you experiment with lengths, shapes, and embellishments!

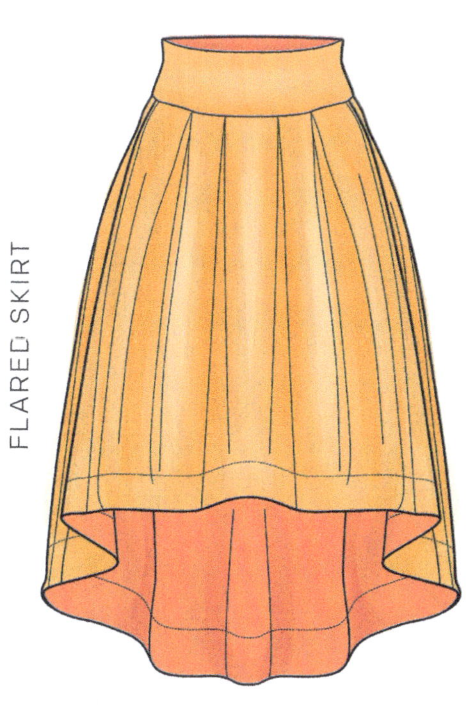

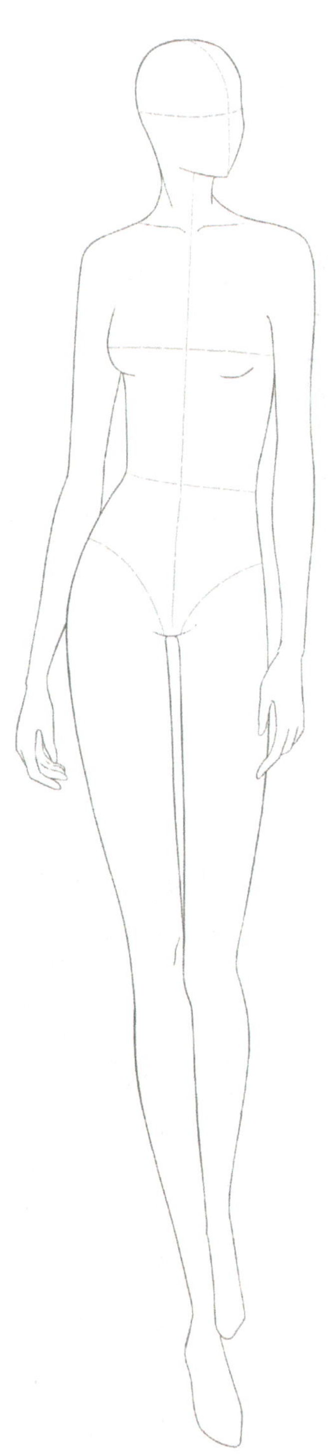

HOW TO SKETCH *Tops*

STEP 1: BEGIN WITH THE SHAPE

Start by sketching the outline of your top, paying special attention to the shape and fit. For instance, if you decide on a large summer blouse, imagine a loose and flowy silhouette that's perfect for hot days.

STEP 2: ADD SPECIAL TOUCHES

Make your top design unique by adding special details. Consider a wide neckline like a boat neck or a deep V-neck to capture the summery feel. Experiment with different sleeve styles, such as bell sleeves or flutter sleeves, for added elegance and movement.

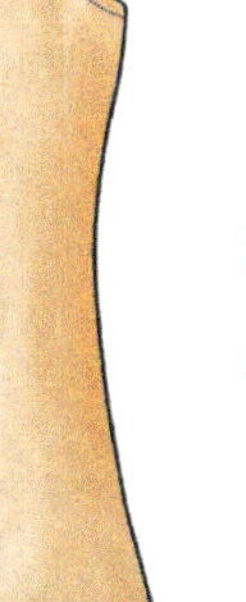

STEP 3: THINK ABOUT FABRIC AND TEXTURE

Again, fabric is a vital component of your garment. If you are working on a design

for a summer blouse, it wouldn't be very practical to make it from a heavyweight fabric like denim or wool; instead, imagine it in lightweight cotton for breathability and comfort. Use shading techniques to show how the fabric drapes naturally, and add texture to your sketch.

STEP 4: PAY ATTENTION TO DETAILS

Focus on the smaller elements that make your blouse stand out. Think about adding delicate lace trims along the neckline or sleeves for a feminine touch. You can also include fabric gathering or pleats for extra visual interest.

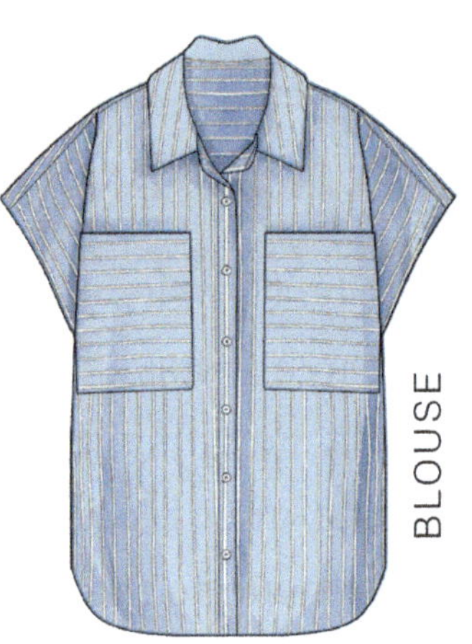

STEP 5: FINALIZE YOUR SKETCH

Review your sketch, and make any necessary adjustments. Ensure the proportions and details accurately represent the nature of your design.

Now, you have all the foundational knowledge to design your own shirts, blouses, and other tops! Feel free to explore different colors and patterns. Happy sketching!

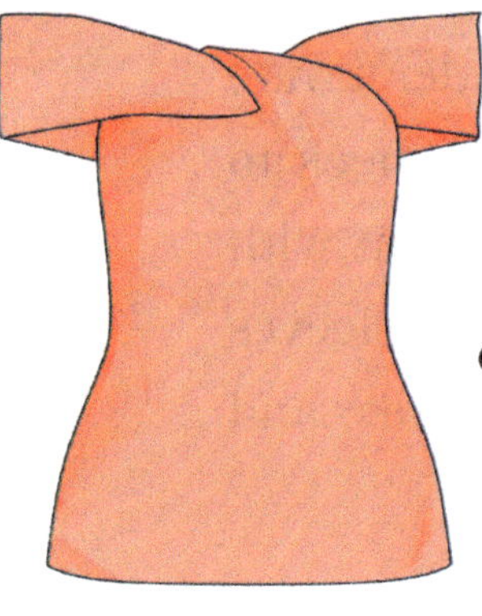

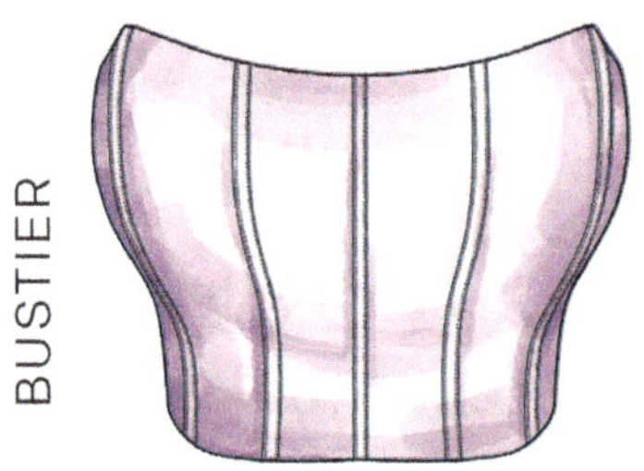

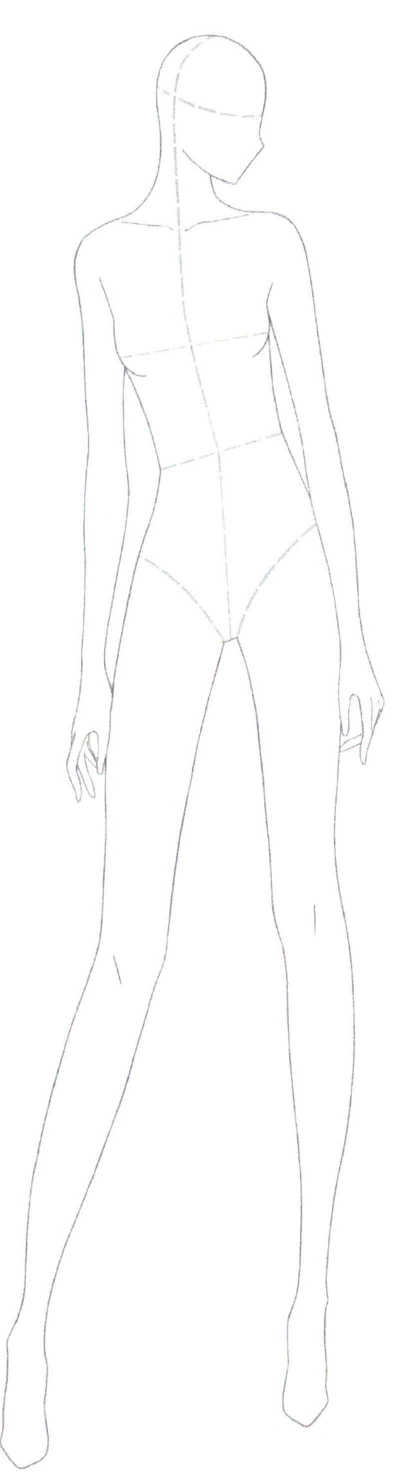

HOW TO
SKETCH
Pants or Shorts

Let's talk about pants! There are so many different types of pants, from tight-fitting leggings to baggy cargo pants. But let's start with a step-by-step guide to sketching your very own pair of trendy jogging pants.

STEP 1: BEGIN WITH THE BASIC SHAPE

Sketch the outline of the jogging pants, including the waistband, hips, and legs. Consider the fit and style you want to portray, whether it's a relaxed or tapered silhouette.

STEP 2: ADD UNIQUE DETAILS

Make your jogging pants stand out by incorporating special elements. Draw an elastic waistband, adjustable drawstrings, and side pockets to give them an authentic look. Consider adding ribbed cuffs at the ankles for a sporty touch.

STEP 3: FOCUS ON FABRIC TEXTURE

Jogging pants are often made of soft, comfortable materials like cotton or fleece. Add texture to your sketch by using shading techniques to indicate the fabric's texture. Consider adding details like stitching lines to mimic the seams.

STEP 4: PAY ATTENTION TO THE DETAILS

Focus on the small details that make each pair of jogging pants unique. Think about the placement and size of the pockets, as well as any decorative elements like logos or patterns. Consider adding contrasting panels or stripes along the sides for an extra style element.

STEP 5: REFINE AND FINALIZE

Review your sketch, and make any necessary adjustments. Ensure the proportions are accurate, and refine the details to make your jogging pants look even more realistic. Add shading or highlighting to create depth and dimension.

Now, you're ready to rock your fashionable jogging pant designs!

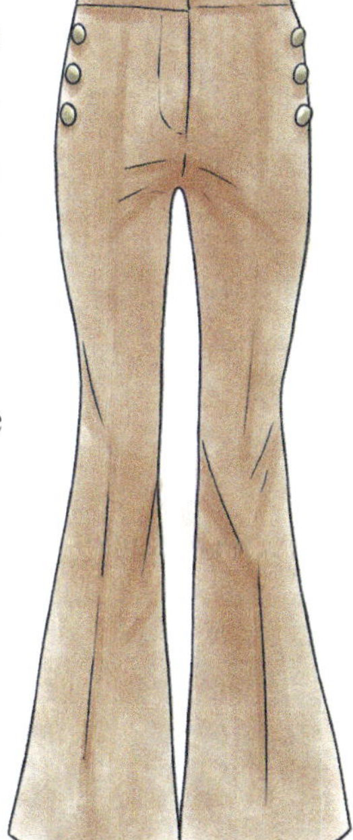

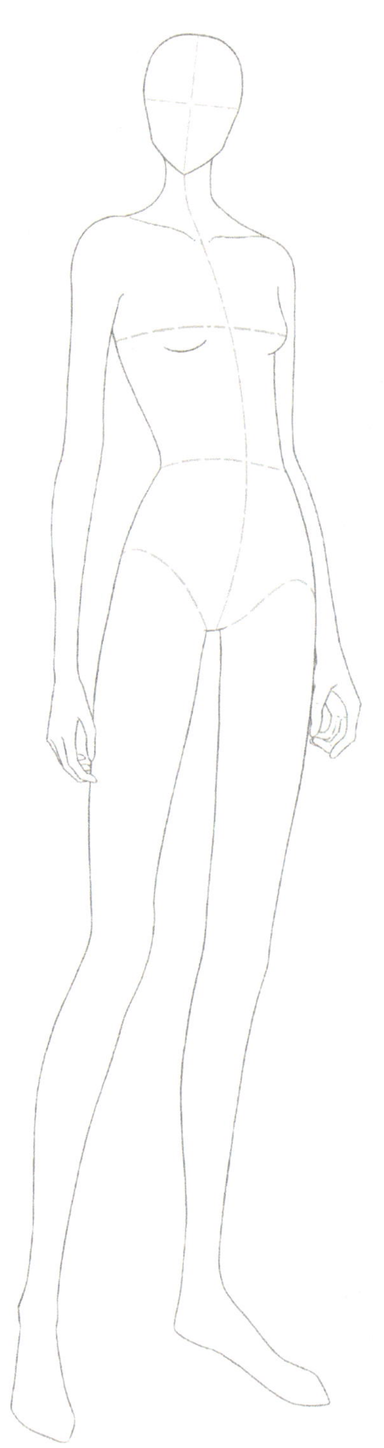

HOW TO
SKETCH
a Jacket or Coat

Jackets and coats keep you warm and protected during winter. Depending on your area, you can also include lighter options like blazers or spring/summer jackets in your collection. Let's focus on a men's down jacket and its design.

PARKA

STEP 1: BEGIN WITH THE BASIC SHAPE

Start by sketching the silhouette of the men's down jacket, capturing its cozy and insulated shape. Think about practicality and style for the winter season.

BIKER JACKET

STEP 2: ADD UNIQUE DETAILS

Make your design unique by adding special elements. Consider a soft collar, a removable hood, and a front zipper with a protective flap. Experiment with different pocket styles, like zippered or flap pockets, to balance functionality and style.

STEP 3: CONSIDER FABRIC FUNCTIONALITY

Choose a fabric that is durable and water-resistant to withstand winter weather. Use shading to show the quilted pattern and texture of the jacket, representing its warm down insulation.

STEP 4: PAY ATTENTION TO THE DETAILS

Consider the small details that make each jacket special. Think about adjustable cuffs, drawstrings for a personalized fit, or reflective accents for visibility in low light. Place pockets, zippers, and any branding elements thoughtfully.

STEP 5: REFINE AND FINALIZE

Review your sketch, and make any necessary adjustments to ensure the proportions accurately reflect a men's down jacket. Add shading, highlights, or patterns to bring your design to life, highlighting the fabric's texture and functionality.

Now, you're ready to create your own outstanding designs for men's down jackets!

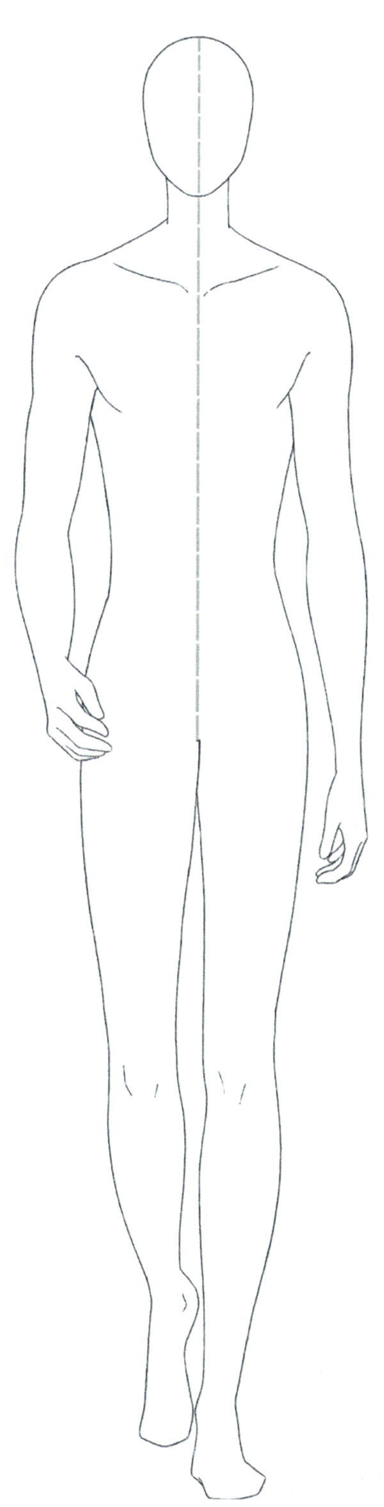

ACCESSORIES

Accessories **are a** vital part of fashion design, and no collection is complete without them. They have the power to enhance any outfit and make a statement. Fashion designers know the importance of accessories and often create them alongside their clothing collections.

Accessories can come in many different forms, from jewelry and belts to shoes, hats, and bags. They add personality and style to an outfit, and they can also transform a look from casual to formal or from day to evening wear. A simple outfit can be elevated with the right accessories, making it more sophisticated and fashionable.

For a fashion collection, accessories can also serve as a unifying element, bringing together different pieces and creating a cohesive look. They can tie together different color schemes or themes, and they can add interest and depth to a collection as a whole.

So, next time you're putting together an outfit, don't forget about the power of accessories!

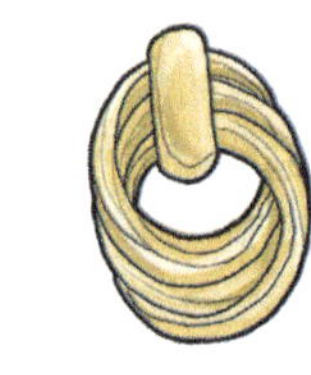

HOW TO
SKETCH
Shoes

When it comes to designing shoes, using a foot template is super important! It helps ensure that the shoe fits just right and makes it easier to draw the lines and curves. Lucky for you, we've got angled-, side-, and back-view shoe templates ready to go.

Let's start sketching some high heels! Take a shoe you have at home, and check out how it's made. This will help you understand all the different parts.

1 First, draw the sole, heel, and basic shape of the shoe. Use light lines that you can see through. Don't worry too much about being perfect.

2 Now, add more details to the top of the shoe—the part that covers the sole and heel. You can get creative and add straps, cute bows, or any decorations you like!

3 Depending on the kind of shoe, you will need to think about how you want to fasten them. For many shoes, laces are the go-to fastening option, but you may want to consider a small buckle or even leaving them as slip-ons with no fastening element!

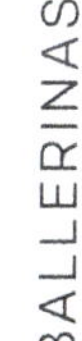

4 Let's make your shoe design even more awesome! Add small stitches to make it look real. And if you want to try something fun, experiment with patterns or other cool details like bows, straps, double stitchings, cut-outs, and more.

5 When you're happy with your sketch, use darker lines to go over your drawing. This will make it stand out and look even better.

6 To finish off your shoe design, add some color! You can even try adding patterns to make it extra special.

Enjoy designing your shoes!

 LET'S DESIGN THE PERFECT PAIR OF SHOES!

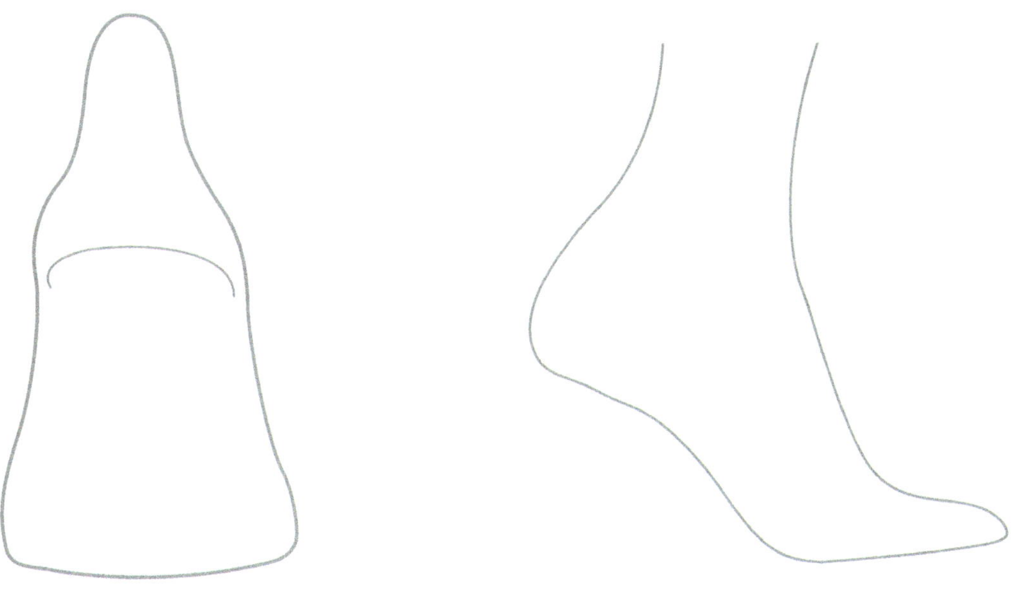

BACKSIDE VIEW

SIDE VIEW

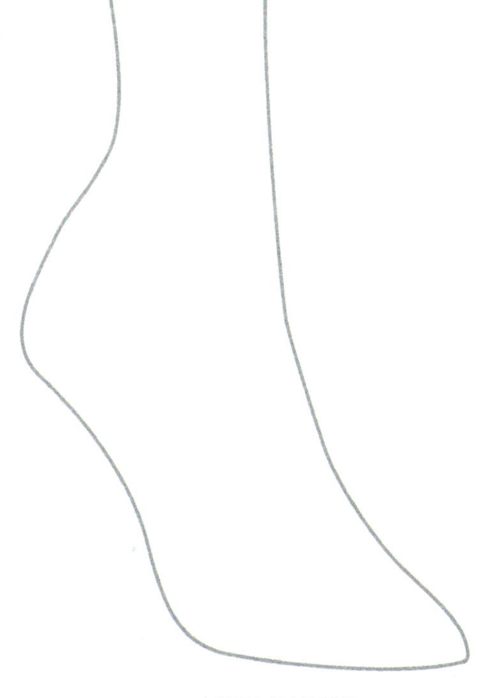

ANGLE VIEW

HOW TO
SKETCH
a Bag

Drawing a bag requires understanding how to put 3D shapes onto paper in two dimensions and paying attention to detail. You can learn how to draw a top handle bag by following these steps:

1 Begin by lightly sketching the general outline of the bag. Remember to use gentle pressure on the pencil. This initial outline will help you position the bag correctly on the paper and determine its dimensions.

2 Refine the shapeless lines into a recognizable bag form. Start by drawing the flap of the bag, and add the vertical strap with the buckle. Keep the lines light as you indicate the placement and shape of the bag's details.

3 Now, add the handle and all the small details that make the bag

unique. Take your time to capture the specific features of the bag you're drawing.

4 When you're satisfied with the overall shape and details, you can draw darker lines over your sketch lines to give the bag more definition. You can also add shading to create depth and realism. To make the bag look more authentic, draw dashed lines to represent stitchings.

By following these steps, you'll be able to create a basic drawing of a top handle bag. Remember to practice regularly and explore different styles and perspectives to enhance your drawing skills further.

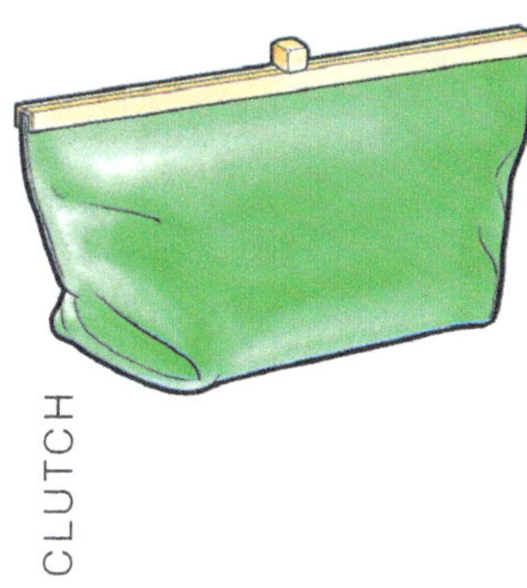

SKETCH YOUR STATEMENT BAG MASTERPIECE!

HOW TO SKETCH *Hats*

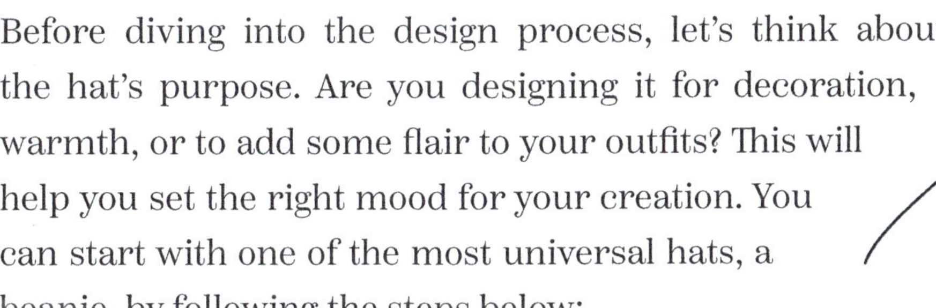

Before diving into the design process, let's think about the hat's purpose. Are you designing it for decoration, warmth, or to add some flair to your outfits? This will help you set the right mood for your creation. You can start with one of the most universal hats, a beanie, by following the steps below:

1 Start by drawing a rounded shape to represent the wool beanie. Imagine a semicircle that covers the top part of the head.

2 Make the beanie look more realistic by adding a curved line below the top edge, slightly inside the circle.

3 Draw another curved line for the bottom edge of the beanie, following the shape of the circle but slightly wider.

4 Create a fold on the beanie by drawing a curved line inside the bottom edge, parallel to the first line you drew.

5 Add texture to the beanie by sketching short, curved lines or small "v" shapes all over the surface. This will show the knitted pattern of the wool.

6 Erase any unnecessary lines to clean up the sketch and make the beanie look neat.

7 Step back and admire your wool beanie sketch! You can add color or shading if you'd like, or keep it as a black-and-white design.

Remember to practice and have fun! Feel free to experiment with different shapes and styles to create your own unique wool beanies. Enjoy your sketching!

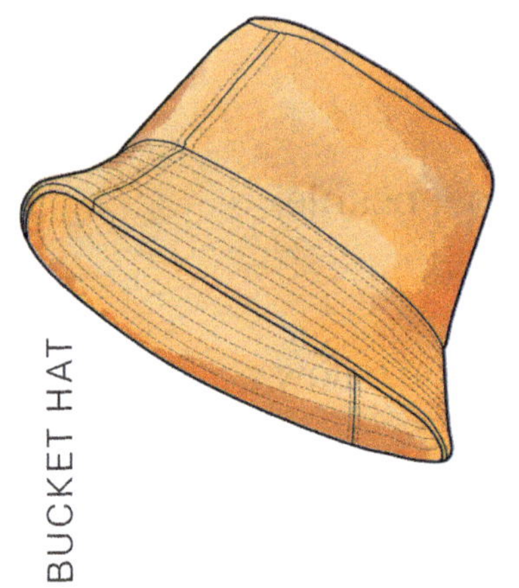

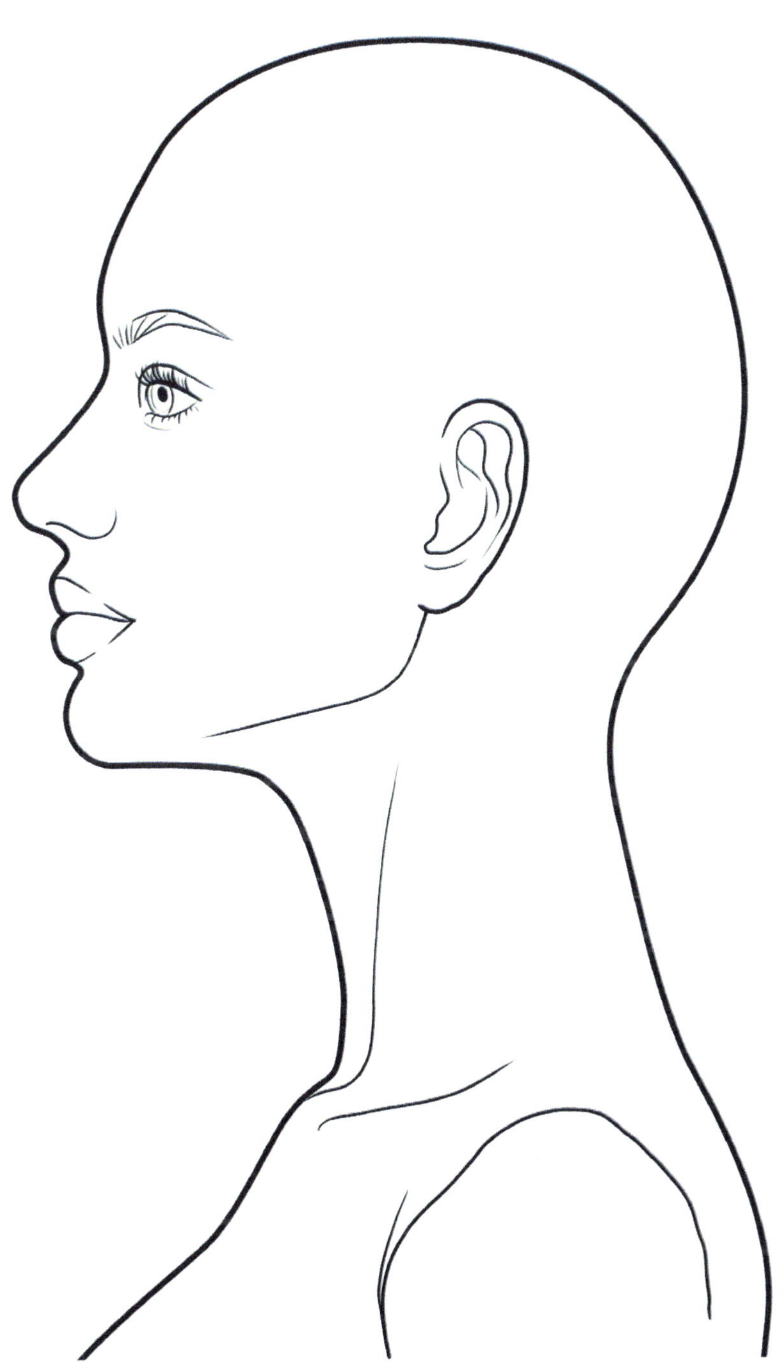

HOW TO SKETCH *Jewelry*

Jewelry design is exciting because you have so many materials to work with. Fine jewelry is often made of 18-karat gold and diamonds or other precious stones.

But there are also fashionable options using materials like brass, pearls, semiprecious stones, cords, and more affordable choices. The possibilities for jewelry designers are limitless, no matter its size!

Today, we'll guide you in sketching a flower ring step by step. Let's get started!

1 Using a hand template such as the one on the following page, begin by drawing the ring shape and deciding on the thickness of the band.

2 Lightly sketch a flower on top of the ring. You can choose any flower you like, just make sure it looks connected to the ring.

3 Add darker lines to define the flower's details. Then, color the ring keeping in mind what material you might like it to be made from. You can also experiment with shading and highlights for extra depth.

If you're up for it, try adding a matching bracelet to the template as well.

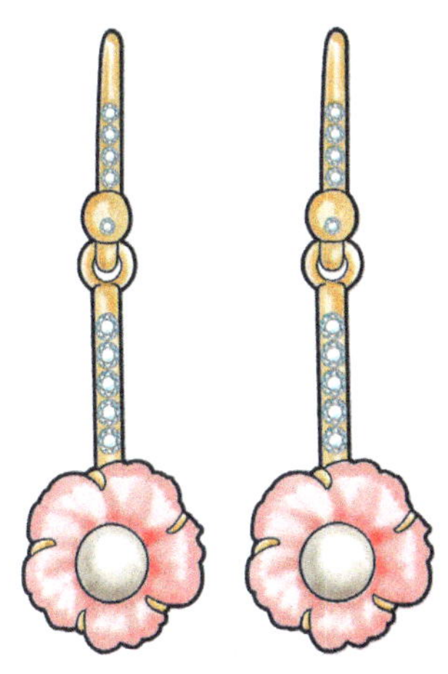

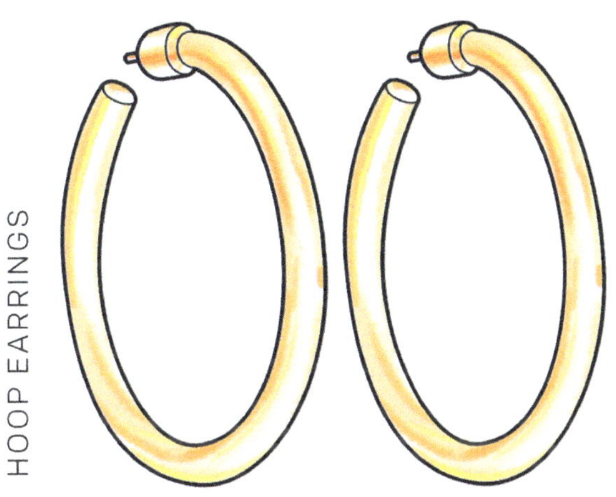

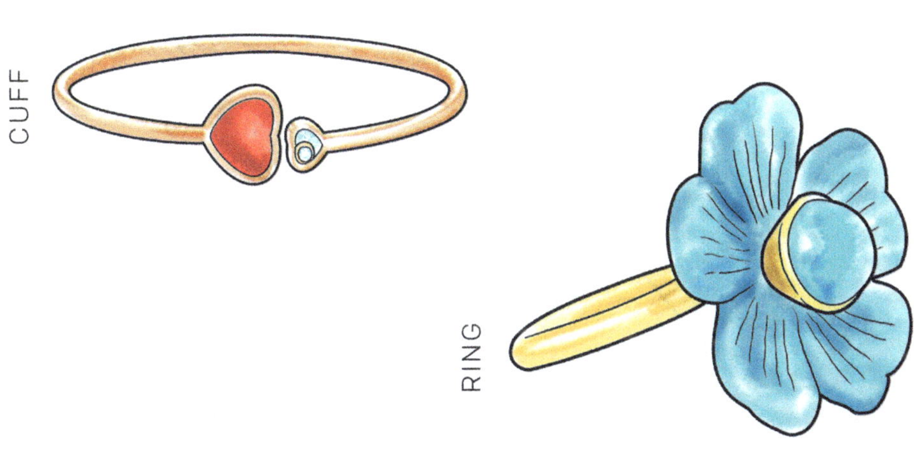

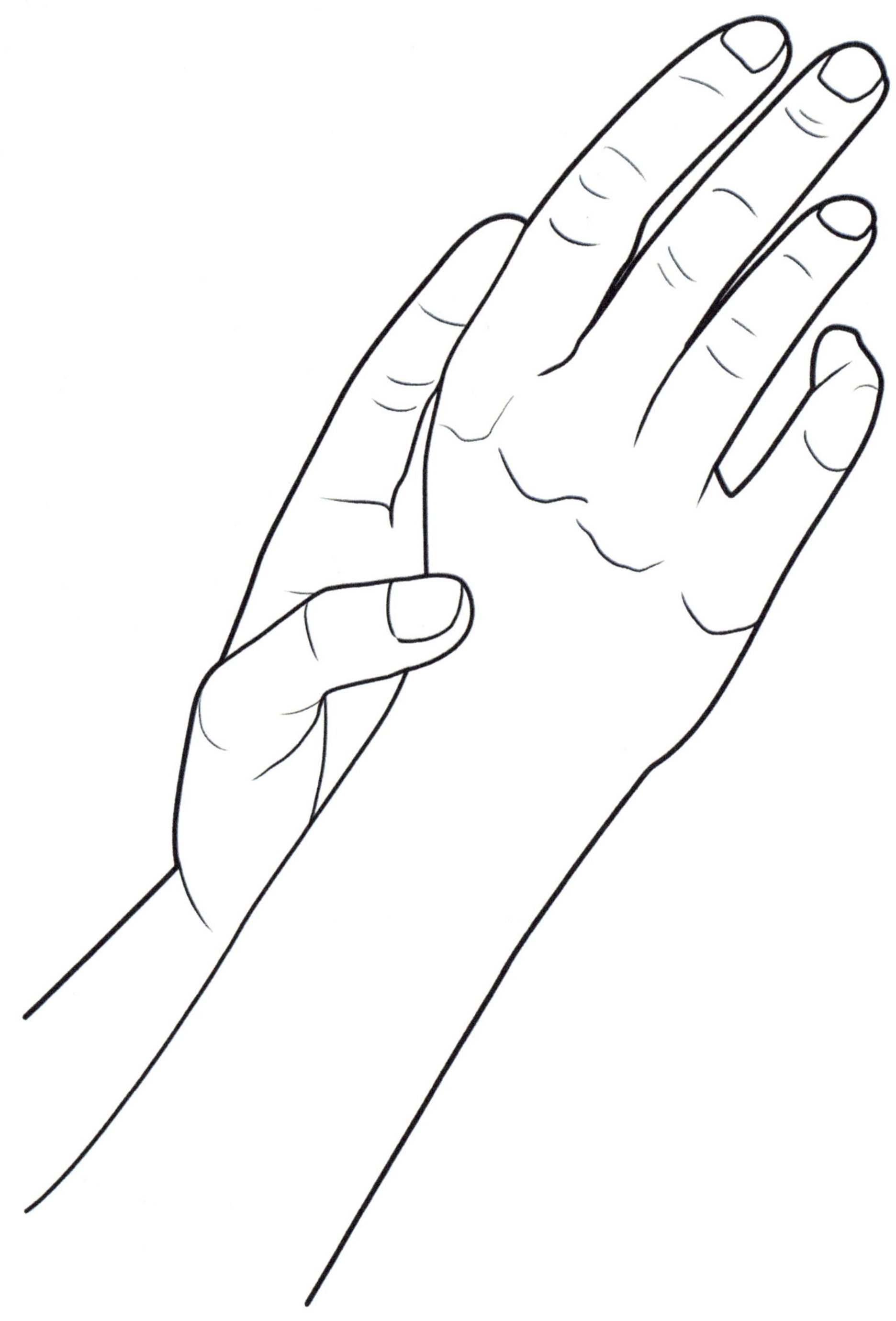

05
Practice
MAKES PERFECT!

The best way to develop your fashion design skills is to practice! You have already started working on your drawing and design skills in this book, but remember that you can practice anywhere. Try taking inspiration from the world around you, including clothes you see people wearing on the street, in magazines, and on TV. Write down your ideas so that you can draw them when you have time.

FASHION DESIGN TIP:
Your drawings and sketches don't have to be perfect, and many of your ideas will change completely. This is all part of the process of becoming a fashion designer: trial and error!

Discovering YOUR FASHION COLLECTION THEME

In the exciting world of fashion design, finding the perfect theme for your collection is like unlocking a treasure trove of creativity. To begin, explore your interests, hobbies, and the things that make you feel inspired. Your theme could be inspired by anything from vibrant street art to majestic ocean waves or even the enchanting world of fairy tales. For example, imagine if you were inspired by the daring and rugged spirit of cowboys: You could immerse yourself in the imagery of the Wild West, collecting images of cowboy hats, leather boots, and fringed jackets. Likewise, you might select warm, earth-toned colors and rich denim blues that evoke the essence of the theme. This cowboy-inspired theme would then guide and inspire your designs, infusing them with a distinctive flair.

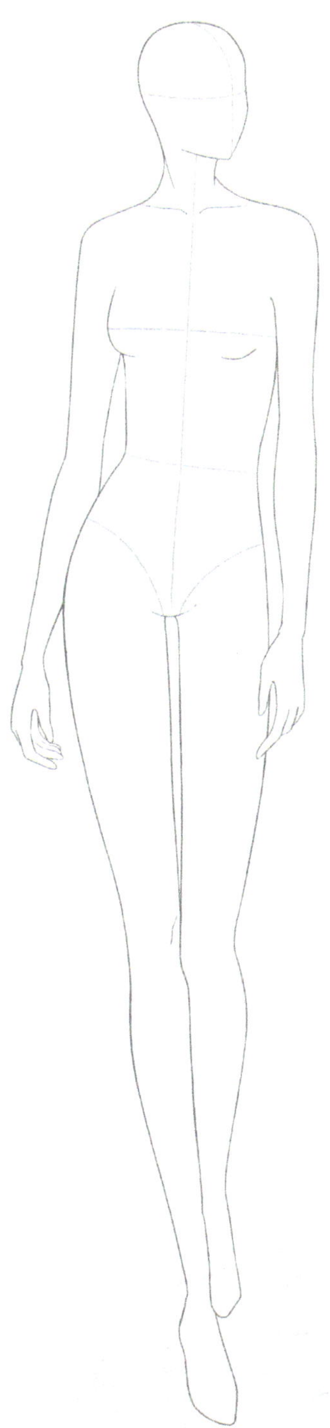

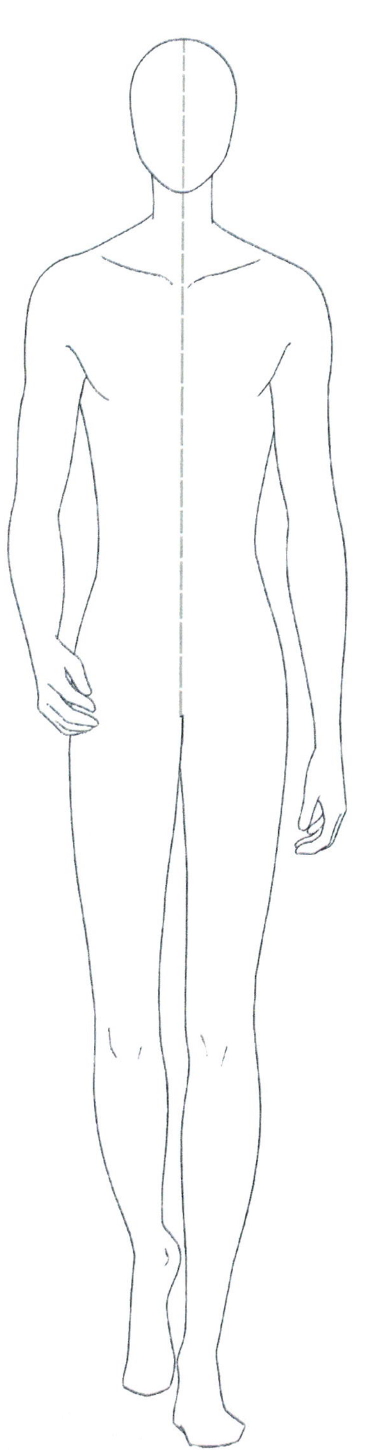

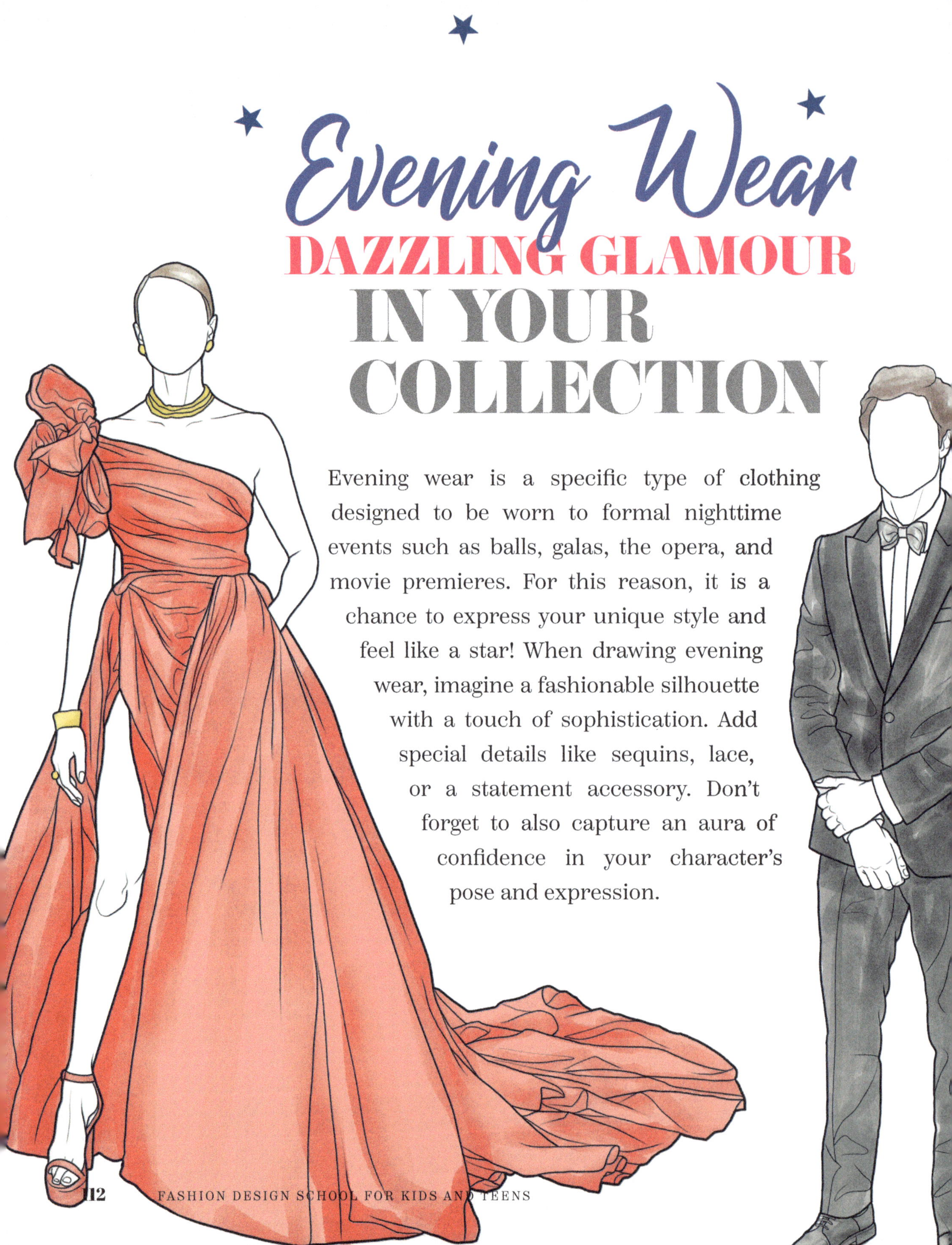

Evening Wear
DAZZLING GLAMOUR IN YOUR COLLECTION

Evening wear is a specific type of clothing designed to be worn to formal nighttime events such as balls, galas, the opera, and movie premieres. For this reason, it is a chance to express your unique style and feel like a star! When drawing evening wear, imagine a fashionable silhouette with a touch of sophistication. Add special details like sequins, lace, or a statement accessory. Don't forget to also capture an aura of confidence in your character's pose and expression.

SKETCH TWO STYLISH EVENING LOOKS

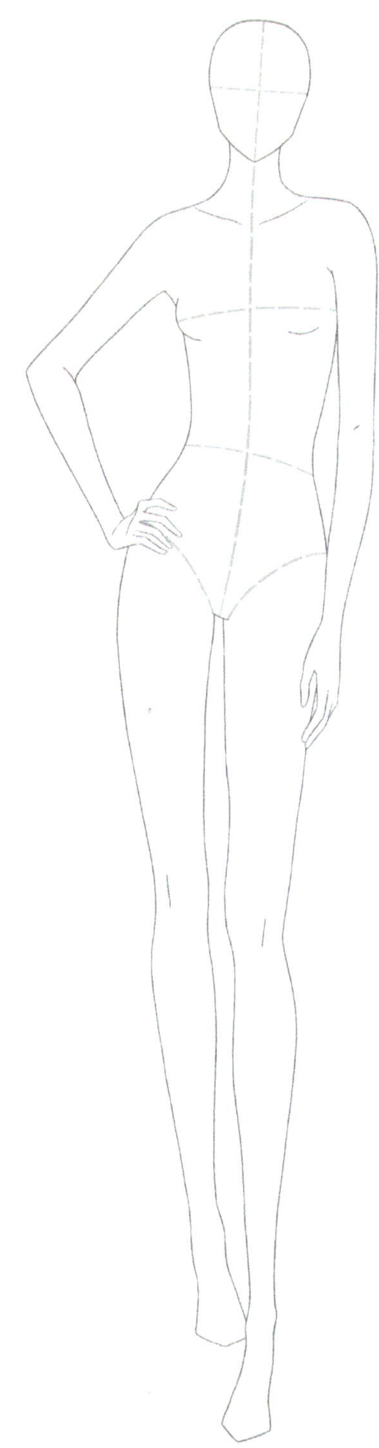

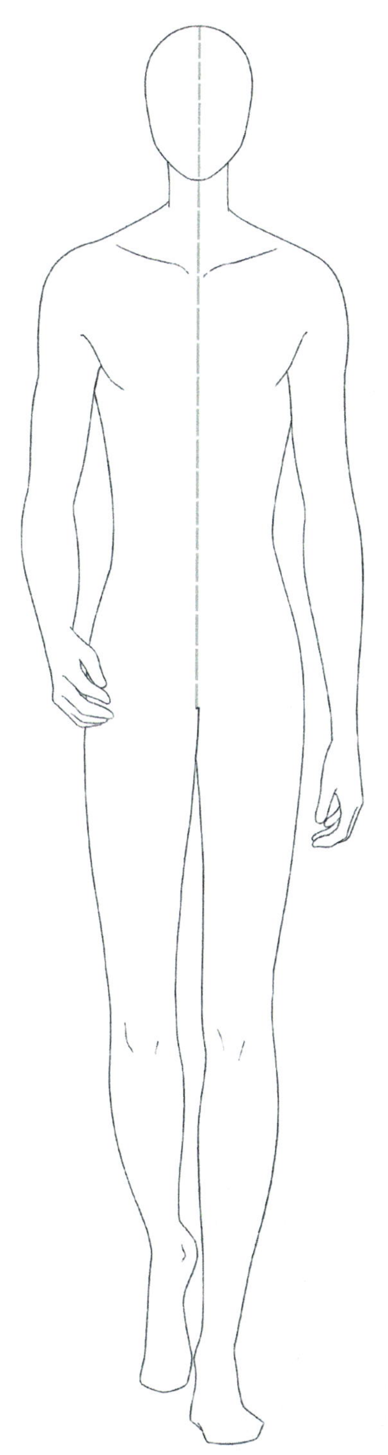

FROM THE STREETS TO THE RUNWAY

Street styles and youth culture have an immense influence on the fashion world. This is demonstrated by the rise of hoodies, which were once a symbol of skateboarding and hip-hop culture but are now a must-have item in everyone's wardrobe. From the streets to the runways, these comfortable yet stylish garments have left an indelible mark on fashion.

As a future fashion designer, it's important to stay up-to-date with the latest street trends that catch your eye. Take some time to explore street fashion trends that catch your eye. Look for inspiration in magazines, online platforms, or by observing people on the streets firsthand. Notice the bold patterns, vibrant colors, and unique accessories that define street style.

Now, it's time to put your creativity to work and create your own street-style-inspired looks!

SKETCH TWO LOOKS INSPIRED BY STREET STYLE

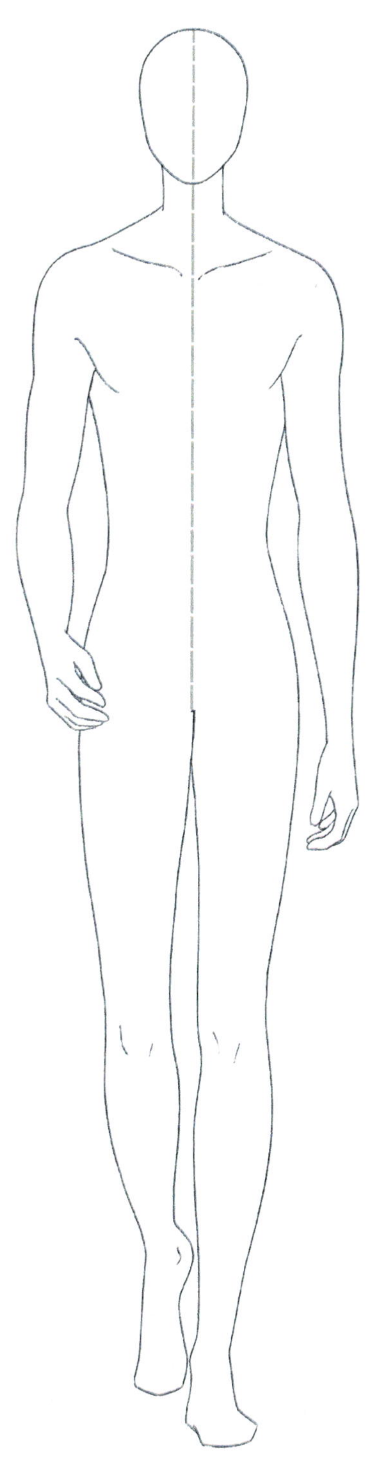

SKETCHING *Fashion* for Every Season

Fashion collections are crafted to cater to the diverse seasons. Designers select materials and styles that harmonize with each climate and season throughout the fashion calendar.

From lightweight fabrics and vibrant colors for summer to cozy knits and warm hues for winter, each collection ensures that fashion adapts seamlessly to ever-changing seasons.

CREATE A CHIC SUMMER LOOK

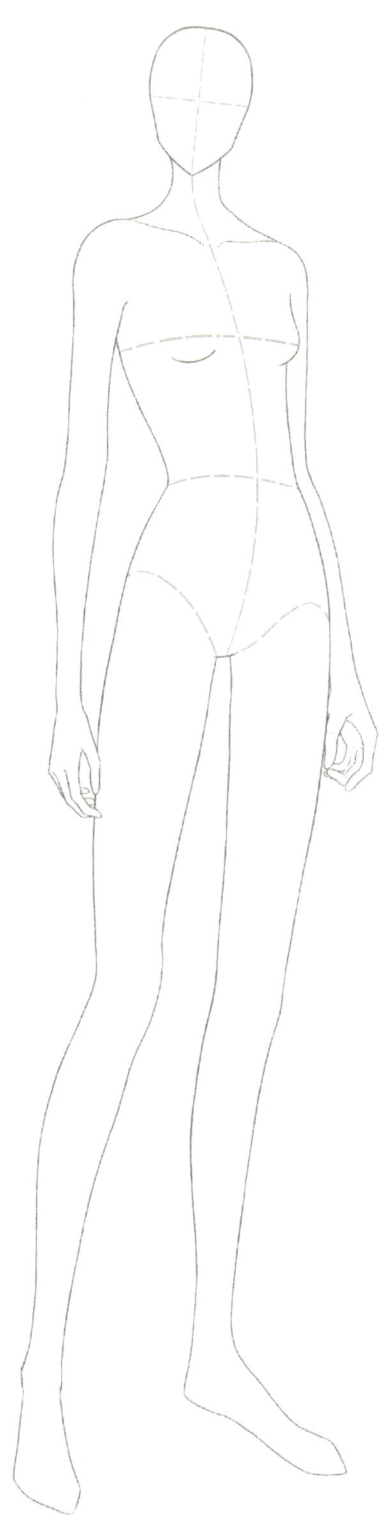

COMPLETE *the Look*
WITH STATEMENT ACCESSORIES

Accessories are essential for adding style and personality to a look. A statement bag can elevate even the simplest outfit, while a pair of trendy sneakers can provide a desired contrast to an evening look. There are no limits, and it can be so much fun to explore some bold ideas.

Don't be shy, and sketch some stylish looks with awesome statement accessories.

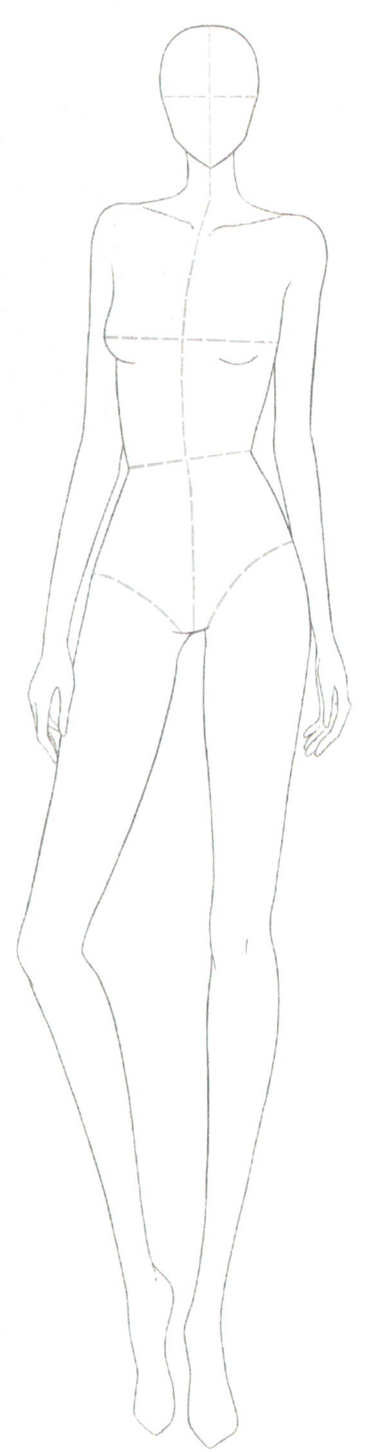

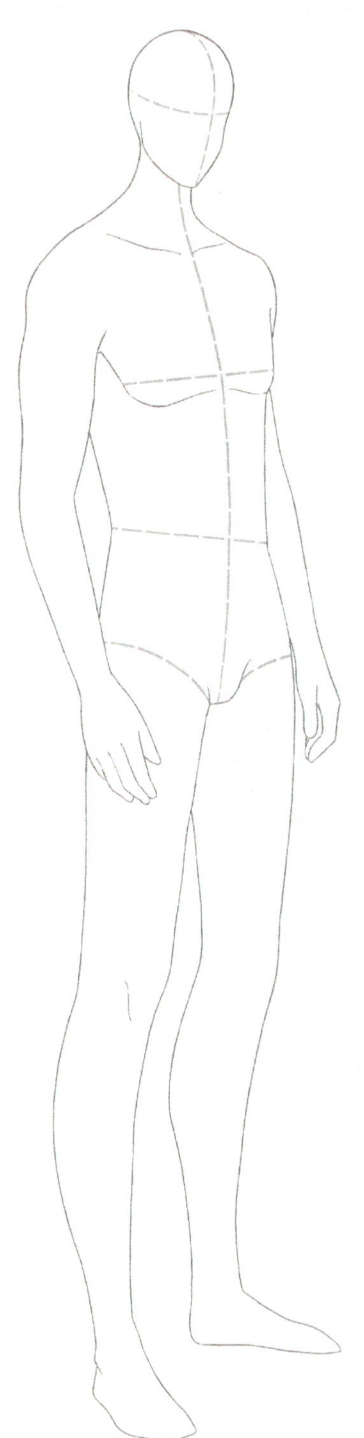

SKETCH TWO LOOKS AND ADD SOME STATEMENT ACCESSORIES

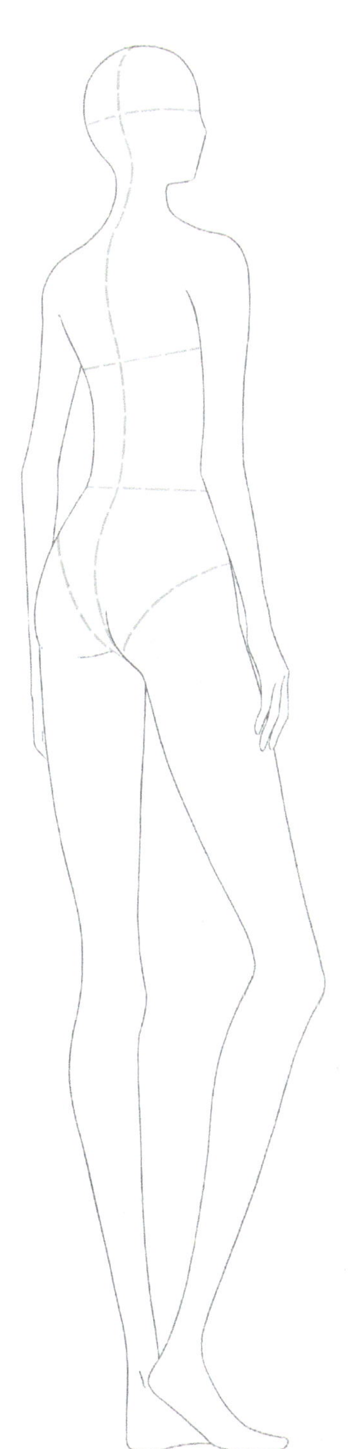

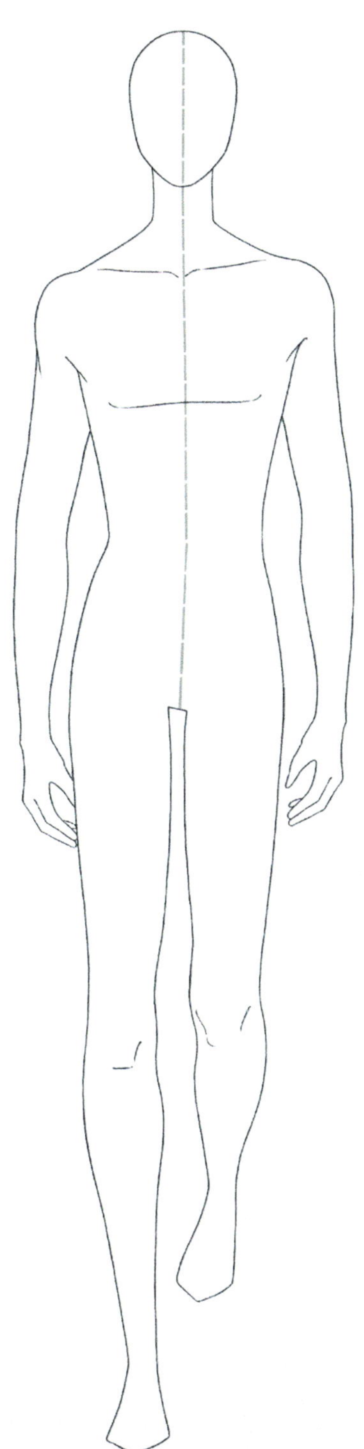

06

PREPARING YOUR *Fashion Week* COLLECTION

You're making excellent progress on your fashion design journey; well done for getting this far! Now, you're ready to put all your new skills into action by designing your very first Fashion Week collection.

Using your new skills, you can sketch your ideas, put together a mood board, choose colors and fabrics, and get designing! You've practiced drawing different items of clothing and accessories, and you probably already have an idea of the styles and designs you like.

Now, it's time to pick up a pencil and design your first collection.

Take your time, and remember to sketch your designs in pencil first before adding markers or fabric swatches, so you can always make changes and improvements along the way. The catwalk is waiting!

BRAND NAME:

SEASON:

DESIGN YOUR BRAND LOGO

DESCRIBE YOUR COLLECTION THEME

MOOD BOARD

PATTERN DESIGN

BAGS AND SHOES

LOOK #1

LOOK #1

LOOK #2

LOOK #3

LOOK #3

LOOK #4

LOOK #5

LOOK #7

LOOK #7

LOOK #8

LOOK #9

LOOK #10

Congratulations!

Now that you have completed this book, you can officially call yourself a fashion designer! You should be very proud of your catwalk collection. Remember that the world's most successful fashion designers were your age once, dreaming of their first fashion collection, and you've already designed yours; how impressive is that!

Fashion is all about having fun and trying different things. Why don't you organize a catwalk show with your friends? Maybe, you could ask a responsible adult to take you to a local thrift store, where you can find the perfect outfits for your friends to model.

FASHION DESIGN TIP:
Don't forget to always carry a pencil and a notebook with you, so if inspiration strikes, you're ready!

BYE BYE

STUDIO

Hey there, awesome reader!

We really hope that this book has taught you a bunch of cool things about the fashion world and made you even more excited about fashion. We've got a special surprise for you in the form of a QR code on this page. All you need to do is scan it with your smartphone's camera, and it will unlock a whole world of fashion figure templates. These templates will help you practice and get better at creating your own fashion designs.

We can't wait to see the incredible designs you come up with! Share them with us on social media using the hashtag, *#ByeByeFashionSchool*. You'll also get to connect with a bunch of other fashion enthusiasts who love fashion just as much as you do.

Keep exploring, and enjoy your exciting fashion journey, full of creativity and endless possibilities!

Best wishes,

The Bye Bye Studio team

Made in the USA
Coppell, TX
22 June 2024

33766610R00079